2nd Edition

ACCOUNTING

Learning and Instruction

CLAUDIA BIENIAS GILBERTSON
Accounting Instructor
Anoka Ramsey Community College
Coon Rapids, Minnesota

BA01BA
PUBLISHED BY
SOUTH-WESTERN PUBLISHING CO.
CINCINNATI, OH   DALLAS, TX   LIVERMORE, CA

Marketing Manager: Gregory Getter
Production Editor: Thomas N. Lewis
Designer: Jim DeSollar

Copyright © 1992
by South-Western Publishing Co.
Cincinnati, Ohio

All Rights Reserved

The text of this publication, or any part thereof, may not be reproduced or transmitted in any form or by any means, electronic or mechanical, including photocopying, recording, storage in an information retrieval system, or otherwise, without the prior written permission of the publisher.

ISBN 0-538-61085-9

Library of Congress Catalog Card Number: 90-62766

1 2 3 4 5 6 7 8 9 D 9 8 7 6 5 4 3 2 1
Printed in the United States of America

TABLE OF CONTENTS

CHAPTER 1   Strategies for Teaching Accounting 1

CHAPTER 2   Resources for Teaching Accounting 17

CHAPTER 3   Teaching Transaction Analysis 31

CHAPTER 4   Teaching Journals and Journalizing 44

CHAPTER 5   Teaching Ledgers and Posting 53

CHAPTER 6   Teaching Analysis of Adjustments and the Work Sheet ... 61

CHAPTER 7   Teaching Financial Statements and Analysis 79

CHAPTER 8   Teaching Recording of Adjusting, Closing and Reversing Entries 89

CHAPTER 9   Integrating Computers into Accounting Instruction 100

CHAPTER 10   Teaching Accounting Control Systems: Payroll, Vouchers, and Inventory 109

CHAPTER 11   Measuring and Evaluating Learning Outcomes 125

INDEX 141

CHAPTER 1
STRATEGIES FOR TEACHING ACCOUNTING

Teaching accounting is an exciting, dynamic, and complex opportunity. Foremost, the accounting instructor should be a positive role model for revealing the many interesting aspects of accounting. Accounting education involves the planned sequence of learning activities designed to guide learners through all phases of accounting. Effective teaching of accounting requires that instructors (a) understand the need for and the objectives of accounting education, (b) know learning principles that apply to accounting education, and (c) plan instruction to prepare students for learning. This textbook is designed to help the instructor prepare for these three elements of effective accounting instruction. As the instructor gains experience, more of the suggestions contained in this textbook can be incorporated into each day's lesson.

OBJECTIVES OF ACCOUNTING INSTRUCTION

Accounting is an integral part of a comprehensive curriculum at the secondary and post-secondary levels. Students enroll in accounting for a variety of reasons, ranging from occupational training to personal use. Accounting instructors must be aware of the reasons students enroll in accounting in order to plan effective learning activities which will produce the desired learning outcomes.

Occupational Preparation

Many students enroll in accounting to prepare for initial entry-level employment in both accounting and general office positions. In addition, entry-level accounting and office positions may lead to advanced-level positions in accounting and related areas.

To assure that the accounting program meets career preparation needs, instructors must keep up to date on employment trends and projections. Two excellent sources for career information are the *Dictionary of Occupational Titles* and the *Occupational Outlook Handbook,* published by the federal government. Students should be made aware of these resources and should be taught how to use these publications to obtain employment information.

Job Entry. Entry-level jobs are positions workers obtain without any experience. Job titles, duties, and educational requirements for entry-level accounting jobs vary depending on the level of responsibility, locality, and size of the business. A career ladder is often used to illustrate the jobs a person may encounter throughout a career. Illustration 1–1 shows a typical career ladder, published in *Century 21 Accounting*.

Steps 1 through 3 represent jobs available to students after completion of one year of high school accounting. Students completing two years of high school accounting may qualify for the first four steps of the career ladder. Further education and/or experience is typically required for steps 5 and 6.

The Bureau of Labor Statistics predicts that an additional 92,000 bookkeeping and accounting clerk positions will open before the year 2000.

General Office. Students may prefer to move into related positions such as sales and data processing. Accounting knowledge and skill are helpful or required in most business careers. Therefore, every high school student preparing for a business career has a need for accounting education.

Advancement. Advanced-level jobs are those to which persons advance after gaining experience or additional training. How long a person remains in an entry-level position depends on the person and the job responsibilities. An employee who does well in an entry-level position may be considered for advanced-level jobs.

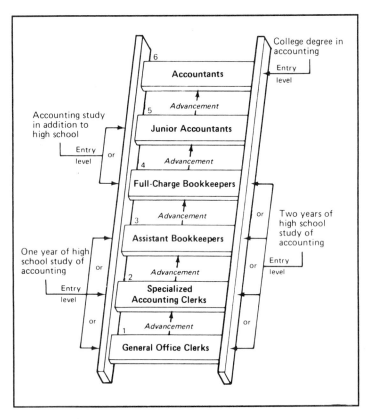

Illustration 1–1 Accounting Career Ladder

Additional education may speed the employee's progress to the top steps of the career ladder.

General Education

A well-planned accounting course also assists students in acquiring many of the learning outcomes appropriate for a comprehensive general education.

Career Exploration. Choosing a career is an important step in every person's life. Since some students want to learn about the field of accounting as a potential career, the first course in accounting, whether at the high school or the collegiate level, should provide career exploration experiences for students. Career information makes the study of accounting more relevant because students see the relationship between what is being studied and the possible jobs they may choose to pursue.

Language of Business. Accounting is often referred to as the language of business. Business employees, as well as owners and managers, need to be able to use this language and must possess knowledge and skill concerning the way financial information is kept, reported, and interpreted.

Personal Use. Some knowledge of accounting will assist all individuals in their roles as citizens, investors, and money managers. Citizens must be able to interpret financial information and understand proposed monetary policy if they are to be intelligent voters and active participants in society. Potential investors must be able to interpret financial information and understand budgets and projections before they decide in which businesses to invest. Finally, every individual who earns a living must plan a budget, keep necessary financial and tax records, and practice good financial controls. Successful completion of an accounting course will help all students acquire skills for personal use.

Communications. Accounting requires precise written and oral communication skills which are useful in both personal and career settings. Students enrolled in accounting will learn how to effectively communicate financial information.

Ethics. The topic of personal and professional ethics is almost a daily issue in today's society. A comprehensive accounting curriculum should include discussions of ethical issues and a study of ethics in accounting.

Mathematics Credit. Many school districts grant mathematics credit for accounting courses. Students receiving mathematics credit for accounting learn a practical application for basic mathematical skills as well as how to interpret mathematical solutions. Correct interpretation assists in making future business decisions.

Community Service

Accounting courses also provide a service to the community. Students who successfully complete an accounting course are granted elective credit toward high school graduation. High school graduates have more job opportunities than non-graduates and are better equipped to participate in community activities.

An accounting course can also serve to retrain displaced employees and/or homemakers. These retrained individuals can re-enter the work force, thereby positively influencing the economy of the area.

Finally, accounting instruction can assist small businesses by providing initial and/or additional accounting training for current employees.

College Preparatory Education

Many students plan to study accounting in college and, therefore, choose to begin their accounting education in high school. Colleges often provide for advanced placement in accounting or credit by examination for high school courses which duplicate courses offered in college. High school accounting instructors must keep up to date on the content covered in the first collegiate accounting course in order to meet the accounting education needs of students planning to continue their study of accounting in college. In addition, high school accounting instructors must maintain communications with local college personnel concerning advanced placement and credit by examination requirements.

PRINCIPLES OF EFFECTIVE ACCOUNTING INSTRUCTION

All instruction requires the use of learning principles. Effective implementation of learning principles increases the likelihood that the desired learning outcomes will be achieved. Nine learning principles apply to the learning process in accounting.

Principle 1—Positive Attitude

> Learning proceeds faster when a learner has a positive attitude toward the material to be studied.

An instructor with a positive attitude toward accounting instruction will encourage students to have a positive attitude about learning accounting. Students with a positive attitude toward accounting will be more motivated to study and understand accounting concepts and principles. Accounting instructors should provide a general overview of the importance and relevancy of the topics to be studied so the students will know why the study of particular topics is important to their development.

Introductory activities can help set the stage for new topics as well as help students anticipate the learning that is to take place and to maintain a positive attitude. For example, an introductory activity for calculating net pay could be a discussion of why an employee takes home less pay than was earned in a pay period.

Principle 2—Knowledge of Goals

> Learning is more effective when a learner knows long-term and short-term goals and objectives.

Long-term and short-term goals and objectives specify what students are to learn, how students are to learn, and minimum performance requirements. Accounting is systematic, with one learner outcome being built on a previous learner outcome. Accounting goals and objectives should follow a similar pattern. Knowledge of long-term and short-term goals and objectives is motivational to students. Learner outcomes should be determined and communicated to students prior to beginning the learning process. Goals and objectives can be repeated throughout instruction to help the instructor and students focus on desired outcomes.

Principle 3—Modeling and Verbalization

> Learning is facilitated when a learner is conditioned for new learning through modeling and verbalization prior to study and application.

Modeling combined with instructor verbalization enhances learning. Accounting instruction can make good use of modeling and verbalization. As journals, ledgers, work sheets, and financial statements are introduced, the instructor can combine a verbal description with a visual model on a transparency or the chalkboard. Demonstration combined with explanation allows learners to see the correct model and behavior and hear the information needed to guide their study and application. Retention is also enhanced by modeling and verbalization.

Principle 4—New Learning Builds on Prior Learning

> Learning is more effective when a learner participates in expanding behaviors where new learning builds on prior knowledge.

The learning process is most efficient when new learning builds on previous learning. In accounting, almost all new learning requires a good understanding of previous knowledge. The instructor must stress this building process by constantly reminding students how the new learning relates to previous knowledge. In addition, the instructor must continuously monitor student achievement of desired learner outcomes to determine if learning can progress or if additional teaching or reteaching is necessary.

One method of tying new material to previous learning is to have students complete a "5-minute write" at the beginning of a class period. In a 5-minute write, each student writes several sentences about what was covered in class the previous day. The instructor then asks students to share what was written until the previous day's topic is thoroughly reviewed. Finally, the instructor summarizes the review and introduces the next topic, stressing the relationship between the two topics.

Principle 5—Individual Guidance Through New Learning

> Learning proceeds faster when a learner is individually guided through each new learning experience.

Most accounting classes are composed of students with varying levels of ability. Learning activities directed to the individual needs of students enhance understanding. Learning occurs as each student is able to process material at a comfortable level. Material too difficult or too easy does not enhance learning.

One method of meeting individual student needs is referred to as self-paced or student-controlled learning. A self-paced approach is one in which students progress individually through course content at their own pace. This approach, however, assumes that students have acceptable reading and mathematical skills and independent work habits. The self-paced approach also assumes that students are able to learn on their own with a minimum of instructor assistance.

A second method of meeting individual student needs places major emphasis on instructor-controlled learning activities directed at meeting the learning needs of each student. In an instructor-controlled approach, instruction is initially directed to the average ability level of the class. Below-average students are given multiple opportunities to learn the material through recycling activities while above-average students are given enrichment activities after content mastery has been demonstrated.

Principle 6—Variety of Materials, Media, and Techniques

Learning is stimulated when a learner is provided with a variety of materials, media, and instructional techniques.

Following the same routine day after day causes boredom and detracts from learning. Variety stimulates students and motivates them to learn. Variety may be accomplished by using any combination of instructional aids and methods discussed in Chapter 2.

In addition to changing the daily routine, the accounting instructor should use a variety of materials and methods during each class period. The attention span for the average high-school student is estimated to be approximately 15 minutes. In order to maintain efficient learning, students should change activities every 15 minutes.

Finally, learning style varies among students. When a variety of activities are used, students will find some activities that match their particular learning style. By using other learning styles, students will strengthen their ability to learn. Teaching styles and learning styles are discussed later in this chapter.

Principle 7—Reinforcement

Retention is greater when a learner is provided with continuous reinforcement.

Reinforcement is the primary mechanism for retention of what has been learned. In the early stages of learning, frequent reinforcement of accounting learning through concentrated drill and practice is required. As learning progresses, reinforcement-type activities may be less frequent. Strong effort should also be reinforced and is especially appropriate for homework assignments. Reinforcement also occurs when the instructor walks by each student at the end of the class period to quickly check and comment on each student's work.

In addition, retention is enhanced when new learning is summarized and related to overall goals and objectives. One method of summarizing new learning is to have students do a "2-minute write" at the end of a class period. Students quickly write everything they remember about the day's topic and are asked to share the writings aloud until all major points are stated. Finally, the instructor should connect the day's topic with the chapter objectives and can also use this opportunity to set the stage for the next day's topic.

Principle 8—Knowledge of Progress

Learning proceeds faster when a learner is aware of progress toward desired outcomes.

Students need to know that they are making progress toward desired goals and objectives. Immediate feedback on student progress is superior to delayed feedback. As learning activities for accounting move from the simple to the complex, what and how well something is learned in one day may influence how well a student can learn the following day.

The 2-minute write discussed in Principle 7 provides immediate feedback to students regarding that day's topic. Each student can assess what and how well the topic was learned.

Additional feedback should be provided by the instructor and through student self-evaluation. Modeling and verbalization of each new segment of learning, as described in Principle 2, should be followed by drill and practice on the new material. The instructor should provide immediate feedback of correct responses as students progress through these learning activities. Upon completion of an assignment, students should also be provided with selected answers to the problems.

Formal evaluations given at frequent intervals also provide knowledge of progress toward desired learning outcomes and can benefit the learning process. Test results should be communicated to students as soon as possible, preferably the day following the examination.

Principle 9—Transfer of Knowledge

Learning transfer is more likely when a learner is provided with training conditions similar to application conditions.

The transfer of learning to realistic everyday problems associated with student needs is one of the major goals of accounting education. Learning activities must be designed to promote the maximum degree of positive transfer of learning to realistic applications. Providing learning experiences in small segments, followed by experiences which combine a number of learnings into realistic applications, promotes learning transfer. Accounting case studies provide realistic applications for small segments of learning. The use of business simulations as capstone learning activities is one way to provide in-class application under near-realistic conditions.

PLANNING FOR EFFECTIVE ACCOUNTING INSTRUCTION

Planning for accounting instruction includes three steps. First, determine learning outcomes which specify what students must do to successfully complete the accounting program. Second, plan learning activities which are consistent with the learning outcomes and which follow accepted learning principles. Third, plan evaluation techniques which will measure students' performance according to the learning outcomes originally specified. All three steps can and should be completed before the first day of actual student learning takes place.

Clarifying learning outcomes is one of the most important steps in planning for accounting instruction. Learning outcomes should specify measurable student behaviors. Learning and instruction are more easily guided if the behaviors are stated in the form of competencies. Accounting competencies represent those tasks which are measurable through demonstration by students. Education based on predetermined, behaviorally-oriented learning outcomes expressed in the form of competencies is often referred to as competency-based education (CBE).

A number of CBE models are currently used in education. A CBE model that is recommended for an accounting program and was published in *Century 21 Accounting,* is given in Illustration 1-2 on page 9.

Program Goals

Step 1 in the accounting CBE model involves determining program goals. Program goals are general, student-oriented competency statements which take two or more general behavioral goals to demonstrate. Program goals for accounting are:

1. Know accounting as it relates to careers.
2. Know accounting terminology.
3. Understand accounting concepts, principles, and practices.
4. Apply accounting procedures.

Three levels of learning are associated with accounting education—knowledge, understanding, and application. Knowledge represents the lowest level of learning and involves learning outcomes which demonstrate recall of previously learned subject matter. Measurement of knowledge in accounting may be through objective-type examinations. For example, knowledge may be demonstrated through matching questions which have students match accounting terms with definitions.

Understanding assumes the knowledge level of learning and goes one step beyond the simple remembering of material. Measurement of understanding in accounting may also be through objective-type examinations. For example, understanding may be demonstrated through multiple-choice questions which have students distinguish between a number of alternatives.

Application involves the ability to perform in realistic situations. Application represents a higher level of learning than either knowledge or understanding. Measurement of the application level of learning is usually through problem-type examinations. For example, application may be demonstrated by having students complete a problem which requires knowledge and understanding of accounting concepts, principles, and practices. Students might be able to answer questions about preparing a report; however, application ability can be measured only by having students actually prepare the report.

General Behavioral Goals

Step 2 in the accounting CBE model involves specifying general behavioral goals. General behavioral goals are student-oriented behavioral statements which require one or more terminal performance objectives to demonstrate. General behavioral goals delineate the behaviors specified for each program goal. Examples of the general behavioral goals for program goal 4 appear on page 10.

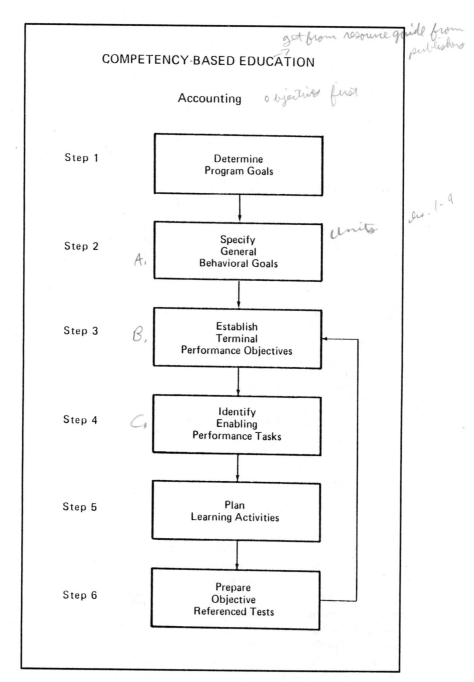

Illustration 1-2 Competency-Based Education Model

PROGRAM GOAL

Apply accounting procedures.

GENERAL BEHAVIORAL GOAL

1. Demonstrate accounting procedures for a service business organized as a sole proprietorship.
2. Demonstrate accounting procedures for a merchandising business organized as a partnership.
3. Demonstrate automated accounting procedures for a merchandising business organized as a partnership.
4. Demonstrate accounting procedures for a merchandising business organized as a corporation.
5. Demonstrate accounting procedures for control systems of a merchandising business organized as a corporation.

Terminal Performance Objectives

Step 3 in the accounting CBE model involves establishing the terminal performance objectives. Terminal performance objectives are statements that indicate the behavior students will demonstrate upon successful completion of a learning experience. Terminal performance objectives consist of three basic elements.

1. The *condition* under which the performance is to take place.
2. The *behavior* (things to be done) expected of a student.
3. The *criteria* (standards) used to determine how well the behavior is to be done.

The following is a terminal performance objective for general behavioral goal 5.

GENERAL BEHAVIORAL GOAL

Demonstrate accounting procedures for control systems of a merchandising business organized as a corporation.

TERMINAL PERFORMANCE OBJECTIVE

Given problems covering accounting control systems (Condition), students will perform the following at a minimum of _____ percent accuracy (Criteria).

a. Use a voucher system. (Behavior)
b. Use a petty cash fund. (Behavior)
c. Determine the value of merchandise inventory. (Behavior)

Terminal performance objectives specify the condition, behavior, and criteria required to satisfy the learning outcomes described in the general behavioral goals. The specific criteria (standards) of performance must be determined by each school to allow for differences in student abilities, job requirements, and local school/community conditions.

Terminal performance objectives specify the minimum level of performance needed to demonstrate successful completion of a block of subject matter. The minimum level of performance may be related to grading standards or to employment standards. For example, a minimum of 75 percent of the behavior specified in the terminal performance objective may meet school requirements for a grade of C. A higher minimum level may be required to meet minimum acceptable employment standards. Many schools now require that the criteria specified in terminal performance objectives be based on minimum employment standards. Using employment standards allows schools to better communicate with prospective employers concerning the specific behaviors students have attained and those that may require on-the-job training to meet the minimum requirements of the position.

To establish the minimum levels of performance for employment, instructors must follow local employment standards. The establishment of an advisory committee made up of prospective employers of accounting graduates is an approach often used to determine the minimum levels of performance required for employment. An advisory committee may also be used to review the behaviors specified in the terminal performance objectives. In addition, some state departments of education provide suggested terminal performance objectives for a variety of curriculum areas.

Instructors should prepare a copy of the terminal performance objectives for distribution to students before they begin their study of each part of the accounting program. Each terminal performance objective should be reviewed with students so that they understand the specific behaviors required.

Enabling Performance Tasks

refer to lesson plans

Step 4 in the accounting CBE model involves identifying the enabling performance tasks. Enabling performance tasks are those steps through which a student must go to prepare for the successful demonstration of the behavior specified in terminal performance objectives. The following example shows the enabling performance tasks required to determine the value of merchandise inventory.

> TERMINAL PERFORMANCE OBJECTIVE
>
> Determine the value of merchandise inventory. (Behavior)
>
> ENABLING PERFORMANCE TASKS
>
> When students have completed the study of merchandise inventory, they will be able to:
>
> 1. Determine the cost of merchandise inventory using (a) the FIFO method and (b) the LIFO method.
> 2. Determine the value of merchandise inventory using the lower of cost or market method.
> 3. Estimate the value of merchandise inventory using the gross profit method.

The relationship between goals, objectives, and tasks in the instructional sequence is shown in Illustration 1–3 on page 12.

Learning Activities—Instructional Delivery System for Accounting

Step 5 in the accounting CBE model involves the planning of learning activities. Learning activities are instructor directed activities planned for one or more students so that students may be able to demonstrate predetermined terminal performance objectives.

Learning activities are an integral part of the daily instructional delivery system for accounting. A daily plan will usually include (1) review of homework,

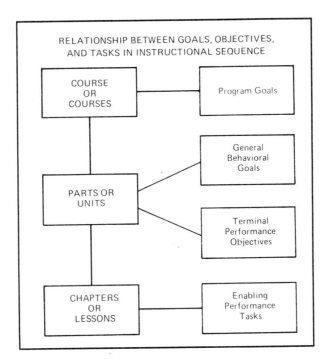

Illustraton 1-3 Relationship Between Items in the Instructional Sequence

(2) reinforcement of prior learning, (3) introduction of new concepts and procedures, (4) demonstration of new procedures, (5) drill of new procedures, and (6) assignment of homework.

Review Homework. If homework was assigned the previous class period, review the homework at the beginning of the period. In order to reinforce prior learning and to provide feedback to students on the quality of the work completed, provide correct solutions to each homework problem. Using an overhead projector with a transparency of the correct solution is an effective way to review homework. Techniques for scoring and grading homework are described in Chapter 11.

Reinforce Prior Learning. Spend some time reviewing prior learning to reinforce the concepts learned and allow an opportunity to clarify any questions students have. Use the review to discuss how the topics fit into the accounting cycle. The 5-minute write previously discussed in Principle 4 is a quick method which can be used to reinforce prior learning.

Introduce New Concepts and Procedures. Introducing new concepts and procedures includes (1) setting the stage for the new learning, and (2) communicating the learning outcomes, long-term objectives, and short-term objectives to students.

Begin each lesson with a general introduction of the topics to be presented. Provide an overview of the need for learning the new material and how this knowledge, understanding, and application will fit in the accounting cycle. Explain WHY the procedure or activity is necessary. A well-planned introduction will establish a positive attitude in students and motivate students to want to learn the material.

Define the learning outcomes and objectives in a sequential manner. Introduce program goals during the first class period of accounting. When beginning a new unit of instruction, introduce the general behavioral goals and discuss how general behavioral goals relate to program goals. Next, provide students with the terminal performance objectives for the topic. Finally, discuss the enabling performance tasks for the segments of accounting to be covered during the class period. For each subsequent class period throughout the unit, present students with the enabling performance tasks prior to beginning any new learning activities.

Instruction during the course should be organized to allow the completion of the accounting cycle several times for several different businesses. The first accounting cycle should involve a business which requires the simplest set of accounting procedures, usually a small service business organized as a proprietorship. Each time the accounting cycle is repeated, a new business should be described and new procedures added. Learning then becomes additive from one accounting cycle to the next.

Demonstrate New Procedures. Introduce all new segments of accounting by demonstrating the new procedure while giving a verbal explanation of the procedure. Give the demonstration and verbal explanation before requiring students to complete application problems on the topic. Students should not be expected to master accounting knowledge, understanding, and application by simply reading textbook material and working application problems. Rather, the study and application of accounting should follow and reinforce what was demonstrated and explained by the instructor.

Accounting practices are guided by basic accounting concepts. Instructors need to emphasize the application of the accounting concepts throughout the course. The following accounting concepts guide the reporting, summarizing, analyzing, and interpreting of accounting information.

1. Business Entity Concept: A business' financial information is recorded and reported separately from the owner's personal financial information.
2. Going Concern Concept: Financial statements are prepared with the expectation that a business will remain in operation indefinitely.
3. Unit of Measurement Concept: Business transactions are stated in numbers that have common values—that is, using a common unit of measurement.
4. Objective Evidence Concept: A source document is prepared for each transaction.
5. Accounting Period Cycle Concept: Changes in financial information are reported for a specific period of time in the form of financial statements.
6. Consistent Reporting Concept: The same accounting procedures are followed in the same way in each accounting period.
7. Matching Expenses with Revenue Concept: Revenue from business activities and expenses associated with earning that revenue are recorded in the same accounting period.
8. Adequate Disclosure Concept: Financial statements contain all information necessary to understand a business' financial condition.
9. Historical Cost Concept: The actual amount paid for merchandise or other items bought is recorded.

10. Realization of Revenue Concept: Revenue is recorded at the time goods or services are sold.
11. Materiality Concept: Business activities creating dollar amounts large enough to affect business decisions should be recorded and reported as separate items in accounting records and financial statements.

Drill New Procedures. Provide drill and practice exercises to reinforce the new learnings which were demonstrated and explained by the instructor. Drill and practice are important to developing accounting mastery and should proceed through increasingly difficult steps until knowledge and understanding can be combined into an integrative application experience.

Chapter 2 of this textbook emphasizes the use of special materials and media to support the learning activities. Teaching methods for the major topics taught in accounting are described in Chapters 3 through 10.

Assign Homework. The homework assignment should serve as a continued reinforcement of the new learnings presented, drilled, and practiced in class. Homework assignments should be varied according to each student's need for recycling, additional learning, or enrichment activities.

When assigning homework, clearly explain the purpose or goal of the homework. When students know the goal of the homework, they are better able to focus attention on the goal and are more likely to benefit from the completion of the assignment.

Objective-Referenced Tests

Step 6 in the CBE model involves the preparation of objective-referenced tests. Objective-referenced tests measure student performance against behavior and criteria specified in terminal performance objectives. Chapter 11 of this textbook is devoted to measuring and evaluating learning outcomes.

OTHER CONSIDERATIONS

Current educational theory supports additional teaching strategies. These strategies can be integrated into the accounting curriculum in a variety of ways depending on the students involved and the educational philosophy of the instructor.

Teaching Styles and Learning Styles

Research has revealed a variety of teaching styles and learning styles. Teaching styles refers to the way or ways an instructor prefers to present new material. Examples of teaching styles include lecturing, involving students in discussions, group problem solving, using paper and pencil-type worksheets, and using tests as a teaching device. Learning styles refers to the way or ways a student best learns new material. Two major learning styles are based on the side of the brain that is most often used to process new information. Left-brained learners process material in a logical and sequential manner while right-brained learners process material in a more global, random manner. Each learner can also be classified as either an abstract or concrete learner.

The challenge to accounting instructors is to use a variety of teaching styles in order to match as many learning styles as possible. In addition, by using many teaching styles, the instructor allows students to gain experience and practice in using alternative learning styles. When allowed to use different learning styles, students will become more proficient in a variety of learning situations.

Many excellent references are available on the subject of teaching and learning styles.

Cooperative Learning

Cooperative learning refers to grouping students together for the purpose of studying, problem solving, and learning new material. Each member of the group is responsible for the level of learning achieved by all other members. Each group is made up of students representing the overall composition of the class, and, therefore, includes above average, average, and below average students.

Several methods of cooperative learning can be used in the accounting classroom. One method would be for the instructor to present the new material as in a traditional class, and then have students work in groups to complete drill and practice exercises and application problems. Each group member helps all other group members prepare for evaluations. Students are tested individually, but each group member receives the average points achieved by all group members.

Research shows that although cooperative learning methods differ, two features are common to successful cooperative learning programs. First, students must work together as a group to achieve a group goal. Second, the success of the group depends on the level of learning achieved by each individual member of the group as opposed to a group product.

Informal methods of cooperative learning can also be incorporated into the accounting classroom. One such method is to allow the above-average student to tutor students requiring additional help. Another method is to encourage students to form study groups to solve accounting problems and prepare for tests, but to evaluate student learning on a totally independent basis. Research shows that the use of study groups does raise student grades. In second-year accounting classes, a group of students can be assigned an accounting problem to be solved. The group must then present the solution to the entire class.

Many excellent references are available on the subject of cooperative learning.

Mainstreaming of Special Needs Students

Many states have legislated the mainstreaming of special needs students into the regular classroom. Mainstreaming has implications for the accounting instructor and the methods and activities used to present new materials.

One way to assist special needs students is for the instructor to tape record all lectures and discussions. These tapes can be checked out by any student for remedial work. (The tapes can also be used by students who miss a class period.)

If a student is seeing impaired, the accounting text can be read and recorded on tape. In many cities, organizations for the seeing impaired will provide this text-taping service. Seeing impaired or physically handicapped students should be allowed to complete assignments on tape or through the use of an educational aid. Tests can also be completed orally.

Most school districts provide additional resources for the instructors of special needs students. In addition, local organizations may provide additional resources for special needs students.

Gifted Students

Gifted students need to be presented with additional challenges in order to maintain a high level of motivation. As mentioned previously, gifted students could be allowed to tutor other students. Gifted students should also be encouraged to seek advanced college placement for accounting or to seek credit by examination. Enrichment-type problems and advanced accounting simulations can also provide extra challenges to the gifted student.

CHAPTER 2
RESOURCES FOR TEACHING ACCOUNTING

The accounting instructor should constantly be looking for new and better materials, activities, equipment, and sources of information to use in the accounting classroom. A new instructor may benefit from using more established approaches whereas an experienced instructor may benefit from new ideas. In this way, the instructor will best be able to effectively implement teaching strategies.

MATERIALS FOR TEACHING ACCOUNTING

A variety of materials are available to assist the accounting instructor. Most of these materials are available from the publishers of accounting textbooks. Accounting instructors should inspect the entire package of supplemental materials offered by a publishing company when selecting a textbook.

Textbooks

The textbook is the backbone of the accounting course. A textbook is used as the primary source of knowledge, understanding, and application of accounting concepts, principles, and procedures. The scope and sequence of an accounting course will be directly influenced by the textbook selected for the course. Therefore, a textbook should (1) provide accounting concepts, principles, and procedures in a logical order; (2) allow students to study and learn at a pace suited to their abilities; (3) provide sufficient drill and practice exercises, application problems, and supplemental problems to support good teaching methodology; and (4) serve as a guide for the instructor in planning instruction.

Textbook selection methods vary from state to state. Some states publish an "approved textbook list," from which all textbooks must be selected. When textbooks are selected from an approved list, a local textbook adoption committee generally recommends the textbook to be selected. In small school systems, the department chair or the individual instructor may select the textbook from the approved list. When a state-wide approved textbook list is not used, local districts are allowed to develop guidelines for textbook selection.

The criteria used to select a textbook should be determined by those instructors who will be teaching the course.

Workbooks

The publisher of the textbook should also publish workbooks to assist students in studying and understanding the text materials. The two major types of workbooks are working papers and study guides.

Working Papers. Working papers contain a compilation of the forms needed to complete the drills, problems, and reinforcement activities in the textbook. In order to be effective, working papers should include forms for all textbook activities. The forms provided in the working papers should agree with textbook illustrations and demonstration transparencies. Although the use of working papers is optional, most instructors feel that working papers save instructor preparation time, student completion time, and reduce the cost of the course. Instructor time is saved because preparation, duplication, and distribution of forms is unnecessary. Student time is saved by having forms partially completed for routine repetitive items involving prior learning allowing students to concentrate effort on new learning. Finally, since working papers forms contain only the number of lines needed, paper is not wasted and costs are reduced.

Study Guides. Study guides are developed to assist students in studying and understanding the materials in each chapter and generally direct students to the important principles of a chapter. Students actively participate in the study of the chapter by providing written responses to study guide questions.

Study guides may be used as (1) chapter assignments to be completed outside of class at the time the chapter is read; (2) pretests to determine how much students already know; (3) diagnostic instruments to guide the instructor in providing additional explanations, supplementary assignments, and special drills; and (4) chapter tests. If the printed study guide is assigned to be completed as the chapter is read, then the same printed study guide cannot be used as a test. If an instructor decides to use printed study guides as tests, some other questions should be used as the study guide as students read the chapter.

Tutorials

The primary purpose of tutorials is to provide additional activities for students who need extra practice or who missed a class period. Usually, tutorials are a computerized, self-paced, interactive review of a segment of the accounting course. Tutorials can be used as an optional activity or can be assigned to students in need of extra drill.

Simulations/Practice Sets

Publishers of basic accounting textbooks also provide a variety of business simulations (practice sets) which combine a number of learning experiences into one capstone activity. Business simulations promote transfer of learning to realistic business applications by combining role playing and problem solving. Students play the role of an accounting employee in a simulated business, solving the problems and performing the activities for a complete accounting cycle.

Business simulations vary in content, scope, and method of completion. Most simulations include journals, ledgers, and financial statement paper. Some business simulations also contain facsimile source documents for all transactions, while others include a narrative description of transactions. Using simulations with the source documents provides students with more realistic experiences because they must work with documents which typify those used in an actual business.

The scope of the business simulation also varies. Simulations are available for service, merchandising, and manufacturing businesses organized as proprietorships, partnerships, and corporations, making their use appropriate after any or all accounting cycles. Practice sets are also available for specific topics such as payroll accounting, pegboard payroll, family finances, and farm accounting.

Finally, computerized and/or manual business simulations are available. Some computerized simulations also provide journals, ledgers, and financial statement paper so that the simulation can first be completed manually before it is completed with the use of a computer.

Accounting instructors use both manual and computerized simulations in a variety of ways. Three common approaches follow:

1. Each student has a copy of the simulation and individually does all work in class. The instructor collects the simulations at the end of each class period and returns them the next class period.
2. Students individually complete the simulation as in the first approach except that work is done both in and out of class. For computerized practice sets, out-of-class work consists of preparing input forms and analyzing results. Instructors often provide check figures which allow students to verify the accuracy of their work as they proceed through the simulation.
3. Students are grouped together in teams with one simulation provided per team. Team members are assigned accounting positions compatible to the simulation activities. Positions might include an accounts payable clerk, an accounts receivable clerk, a payroll clerk, a cash payments clerk, a cash receipts clerk, and an accountant. Students generally rotate through the various positions according to a schedule determined by the instructor.

Scoring and grading business simulations is covered in Chapter 11.

Computerized Problems

Publishing companies produce supplemental accounting problems that can be completed on a microcomputer. In some cases, these problems are the same ones that students have completed manually. When the problems are the same, students should complete the problem manually first and then use the microcomputer to complete the problem. By completing the problem both ways, students can see the similarities and differences between a manual and a computerized accounting system.

Supplemental computer problems are sometimes completed with the use of an electronic spreadsheet program. The problem includes a template, which is a pre-developed electronic spreadsheet. Students use the template to complete the problem. Spreadsheet accounting packages teach students how to use electronic spreadsheet programs, develop electronic spreadsheets, and apply accounting concepts, principles, and procedures to electronic spreadsheets.

Overhead Projector Transparencies

Overhead projector transparencies are essential in accounting. The use of transparencies allows the instructor to model correct procedures during the presentation of new materials. Transparencies also serve as feedback and reinforcement in the review of homework problems. Publishing companies typically provide two types of transparencies or transparency masters.

Teaching Transparencies. Transparencies used to supplement the presentation of new material are called teaching transparencies. Teaching transparencies cover such topics as the debit/credit rules, steps for making a journal entry, steps followed in posting, examples of how to rule a journal, and summaries of accounting definitions and concepts.

Solution Transparencies. Transparencies used to illustrate the correct solution to drills, problems, and supplemental activities are called solution transparencies. Solution transparencies are a vital component of homework review. Students must get feedback as to the correctness of their assignments, and the quickest way to provide this feedback is to display the correct solution on a transparency. Because students need accurate feedback, solution transparencies should be prepared on forms identical to the working papers used by students.

Hypergraphics

One of the newest teaching aids is the use of hypergraphics, or animated transparencies. Hypergraphics are designed to assist the instructor in the presentation of new material. Used in connection with a microcomputer and an overhead projector, hypergraphics allow the instructor to display accounting procedures such as the actual posting of a journal entry.

Demonstration Problems

Demonstration problems are designed to assist the instructor in presenting new material. A demonstration problem is a set of accounting data corresponding to the new material being presented. The data can be used by the instructor to model the procedure being presented, rather than using the textbook example. Demonstration problems give students one more opportunity to see the correct procedure modeled by the instructor. Demonstration problems are usually included in the teacher's resource guide.

Case Studies

A case study is an application problem which uses the application level of learning. Students are given an actual business situation and are asked to suggest solutions to the problem. Case studies can be assigned to individual students or to cooperative learning groups and solutions can be presented orally or in written form. The use of case studies thus incorporates more than the application of accounting concepts. Written communications, oral communications, and cooperative learning can all be integrated into a case study. In addition, case studies can be used to introduce the topic of ethics into the accounting curriculum.

Evaluative Tools

Evaluative tools can be obtained from the textbook publishing company or designed by the instructor. Commercially developed evaluation tools are available in several forms. The use and scoring of evaluative tools is discussed more fully in Chapter 11.

Problem Tests. Problem tests require students to actually complete an accounting procedure such as making journal entries or preparing financial statements. The application level of learning is measured through the use of problem tests, which can be used at the end of each chapter or unit.

Objective Tests. Objective tests typically include true/false, matching, multiple choice, and short-answer questions. Both the knowledge and understanding levels of learning can be measured through the use of objective tests, which can be used at the end of each chapter or unit. In addition, some publishers provide different versions of the same test.

Computerized Test Banks. Many publishing companies offer computerized test banks which consist of an electronically stored "bank" of test questions. Test banks can include multiple-choice, true/false, completion, and problem-type questions. Items can be selected randomly or by the instructor identifying specific questions. Once selected, the questions are arranged in an appropriate format and a hard copy of the test is generated. Some test banks offer the option of rearranging the same items to provide an alternate form of the test.

Computerized Tests. Computerized tests are pre-programmed exams which are completed by students through the use of a microcomputer. Tests completed on a microcomputer offer the advantage of automatic scoring and an analysis of the test items. However, computerized tests are usually limited to objective-type questions. In addition, the use of computerized tests is dependent on the number of computers available.

Miscellaneous Motivational Aids

A variety of motivational aids are also available, including sound filmstrips, instructional wall charts, achievement awards, and accounting rulers.

ACTIVITIES FOR TEACHING ACCOUNTING

As discussed in Learning Principle 6, Chapter 1, a variety of materials, media, and instructional techniques should be used to increase motivation. A variety of activities can also serve to meet the needs of students with different learning styles.

Flash Cards

An instructor-directed drill using information appearing on a series of cards, commonly referred to as flash cards, is an effective change-of-pace class activity used by many accounting instructors. Flash cards can be used as a review or as a reinforcement activity.

A flash card activity should require quick student response to questions raised by the instructor as individual cards are held up for the class to observe. Flash cards are generally prepared in sets designed to cover specific segments of accounting. For instance, one card may be prepared for each of several accounts. As each card is revealed, the instructor may ask the following questions: (1) What is the account classification? (2) What is the normal balance? (3) How is the account increased? (4) How is the account decreased? (5) Is the account adjusted at the end of a fiscal period? (6) Is the account closed at the end of a fiscal period? (7) On which financial statement does the account appear?

Another example is to write an accounting term on one side of the card and the definition on the opposite side. Use one card for each term. The instructor can reveal the term and ask for the definition or reveal the definition and ask for the term.

Games

The number and kinds of games that can be used in accounting is limited only by the imagination of the instructor. Games can be used to reinforce new learning or to review previous learning. Common games are:

1. Definition Bingo — Bingo cards are made with one accounting term in each square. As the instructor reads a definition, students cover the term on the card. Regular bingo rules determine the winner.
2. Jeopardy — Prepare a large board with 3 × 5 inch squares for questions. Have students write answers (such as "amounts owed by a business") on 3 × 5 inch index cards. Attach the index cards to the board with tacks. As an answer is revealed, students must recite the correct question (What is a liability?). Regular jeopardy rules are followed.
3. Definition Bee — Divide class into two groups that line up facing each other on opposite sides of the room. Alternating groups, ask a student either to define a term or provide a term for a definition given. Award one point for each correct answer. Students do NOT sit down because of an incorrect response. (Alternative: Students DO sit down after an incorrect response, but only if the next person on the opposing team gives the correct answer. The team with the last class member standing is the winner.)
4. Transaction Analysis Bee — Similar to definition bee except students analyze a transaction into its debit and credit parts.
5. Football — Draw a football field on the chalkboard with yard lines drawn every ten yards. Divide class into two teams. Alternating teams, ask questions. A correct response moves the ball ten yards. On an incorrect response, the other team can "intercept" by providing the correct response. (Questions can cover definitions, transaction analysis, debit/credit theory, purpose or format of financial statements, etc.)

Although motivational, games take a relatively large amount of class time. In addition, not all students are actively participating all of the time. Therefore, the use of games should be limited.

Paper and Pencil Activities

Paper and pencil activities can be used to reinforce new material or to review previous learning. Some common paper and pencil activities are:

1. Crossword Puzzles—Similar to regular crossword puzzles, but using accounting terms. Computer programs that allow an instructor to develop a customized crossword puzzle are available.
2. Word Search—Accounting terms are arranged vertically, horizontally, and diagonally on a grid. Blank squares on the grid are filled with random letters. Given a list of terms, students search for the terms on the grid. Computer programs are available that create a word search from instructor selected words.
3. Terminology Unscramble—The letters of an accounting term are scrambled and written on paper. The process is repeated for several terms. Students unscramble each group of letters and write the term in the space provided.

Unlike games, paper and pencil activities enable all students to be actively participating throughout the activity.

Form Analysis

Looking at an illustration, or listening to the instructor's description of an illustration, is often ineffective for students. Some students need guidance as they read and analyze textbook illustrations. A set of questions or some guide should be provided to help students see the important aspects of the illustration.

Illustration 2–1 on page 24 is an example of a device which can be used to help students analyze a work sheet form. The grand total of all line totals is provided to guide students to the correct solution. Form analysis drills measure if students understand work sheets, not if students can complete work sheets.

Field Trips

Arranging for a field trip is much the same as planning any instructional activity. All details need to be planned in advance. The purpose of the trip, how the trip relates to the current accounting topic, what students should see, and what questions should be answered must be determined before the field trip. The instructor should visit the business to discuss the details prior to making the trip. Finally, the details and objectives of the trip need to be reviewed with all students.

Once on the field trip, students should be listening for answers to the questions and issues discussed in class. Without pre-field trip planning and discussion, students often are not sure what they should be looking for or asking about. After the field trip, students should participate in a follow-up activity. Suggested follow-up activities include a group discussion, small group discussions with an oral summary to the entire class, or a written evaluation.

WORK SHEET ANALYSIS
6-Column

DIRECTIONS: Circle the numbers of the columns in which each of the accounts listed should appear on a completed work sheet. Add the numbers circled for each account and place the total in the space provided at the right. Add the totals for each line and record the grand total in the space provided. The line grand total should be 90.

Account Title	Trial Balance		Income Statement		Balance Sheet		Line Total
	Dr.	Cr.	Dr.	Cr.	Dr.	Cr.	
Cash	(1)	2	3	4	(5)	6	6
Supplies—Housekeeping	(1)	2	3	4	(5)	6	6
Furniture	(1)	2	3	4	(5)	6	6
Office Equipment	(1)	2	3	4	(5)	6	6
Cleaning Equipment	(1)	2	3	4	(5)	6	6
Northstar Plumbing Company	1	(2)	3	4	5	(6)	8
Steinke Electrical Company	1	(2)	3	4	5	(6)	8
Superior Furniture	1	(2)	3	4	5	(6)	8
Tyler Erickson, Capital	1	(2)	3	4	5	(6)	8
Tyler Erickson, Drawing	(1)	2	3	4	(5)	6	6
Room Sales	1	(2)	3	(4)	5	6	6
Advertising Expense	(1)	2	(3)	4	5	6	4
Laundry Expense	(1)	2	(3)	4	5	6	4
Miscellaneous Expense	(1)	2	(3)	4	5	6	4
Rent Expense	(1)	2	(3)	4	5	6	4
Grand Total							90

Illustration 2-1 Form Analysis for a Work Sheet

Field trips which are beneficial to accounting students include trips to local accounting firms, accounting departments in local retail firms, the school district's accounting department, and data processing centers.

Guest Speakers

Arranging for a guest speaker is much the same as planning for a field trip. All details must be planned in advance. The speaker must be chosen based on both the speaker's experience in the topic area and the speaker's ability to effectively present material.

Students must also be prepared for the guest speaker. Students need to know what topic the speaker will be addressing and how the topic fits into the accounting curriculum.

Students can also prepare for a guest speaker by outlining specific questions they will ask of the speaker. Again, a follow-up activity should be completed.

Shadowing

The purpose of shadowing is to give students a chance to more closely experience specific accounting positions. Shadowing involves having a student "shadow" or follow an employee for an entire day. Ideally, the employee carries on with normal activities, taking time to discuss job responsibilities with the student and allowing the student to ask questions. Shadowing can be done for almost any accounting-related occupation in which a student may be interested. Prior to the shadowing experience, students should be informed of the position they will shadow. This procedure will give the student time to formulate a set of questions to be answered during the experience. As a follow-up activity, the student could give an oral report to the rest of the class.

Mentoring

Related to shadowing, but on a long-term basis, mentoring connects a student with someone in an accounting-related position (the mentor). The mentor serves as an advisor to the student, helping the student make career decisions. The mentor can also help the student establish a network of people in similar or related positions. Obviously, mentoring is designed to assist students interested in accounting as a career.

Accounting for Student Clubs

Second-year accounting students can volunteer as bookkeepers for student organizations. The student organization and the student volunteer will both benefit by the arrangement. The instructor needs to take an active role in monitoring the records of the volunteers.

Study Groups

Research shows that accounting students who utilize study groups to complete problems and prepare for exams, achieve higher grades in accounting. For above-average students, the study group will serve as a review of material and a chance to develop communication skills. In addition, study groups can be used to add variety to the daily accounting routine. The formation and use of study groups (and the sharing of phone numbers) should be encouraged by the instructor.

EQUIPMENT FOR TEACHING ACCOUNTING

A variety of equipment can be used in the teaching of accounting. To effectively enhance learning and instruction, accounting instructors should vary the use of the equipment as exclusive use of only one type of media leads to monotony. Using a variety of media throughout the learning process promotes interest, motivation, and subject-matter retention.

Chalkboard/Whiteboard

One piece of equipment available in virtually all classrooms is a chalkboard. In order to be effective, use a clean chalkboard, use large, legible writing, and plan each complete chalkboard presentation in advance. Classrooms used only for accounting instruction should have a section of the chalkboard permanently ruled with T accounts, ledger accounts, and a general journal. A popular alternative to the chalkboard is a whiteboard, which is used with chalkless, colored marking pens. The whiteboard is cleaner to use, having no chalk residue. In addition, the colored marking pens allow the instructor to use color to emphasize important points.

The chalkboard, used in conjunction with an overhead projector, provides an excellent means of illustrating accounting concepts, principles, and procedures. When used with an overhead projector, material displayed on the overhead projector serves as the primary source of information. Questions from students concerning points which need further explanation are then illustrated on a chalkboard.

Overhead Projector

An overhead projector is extremely useful and versatile and should be available in every accounting classroom. As previously stated, the overhead projector can be used along with the chalkboard for most effective instruction. Using an overhead projector as the primary teaching device is effective for a number of reasons:

1. The overhead projector allows an instructor to face the class at all times during a presentation.
2. Commercially prepared transparencies are available for theory presentations and problem solutions.
3. Instructor-prepared transparencies are relatively easy to develop and may be saved for future use.
4. Transparencies save class time as compared to chalkboard presentations; instructors do not have to spend unproductive time writing forms or materials on the chalkboard.
5. Transparencies of blank accounting forms allow instructors to complete a form step-by-step in full view of the class.
6. Transparencies allow projection of only key points which need special emphasis.

Material not being discussed should not be projected. Using a piece of paper to cover unwanted material, an instructor can build a presentation in segments following a simple to complex format.

Overlays (a series of transparencies) may also be used in combination to build, sequentially, a procedure where each transparency is a subset of the entire presentation.

Instructors using an overhead projector need to consider physical positioning of the projector and screen, size of screen, and size of characters or images to be projected.

Computers

Microcomputers are a valuable teaching resource and learning tool for the accounting program. Integrating the use of computers brings realism to the classroom, increases instructor effectiveness, responds to individual student differences, and builds student motivation. Learning how businesses use computers in their accounting systems provides a valuable learning experience for students. However, students should gain mastery of the various basic manual accounting cycle components before they begin using a computer. The use of computers in accounting is covered in Chapter 9 of this text.

Bulletin Boards/Wall Charts

A bulletin board can be an effective teaching tool to motivate, interpret, supplement, and reinforce new learnings. Effective bulletin boards must be readable from across the room and must be changed frequently to maintain student interest. An effective bulletin board is one which is frequently referred to by the instructor during learning. Examples for the use of bulletin boards are given throughout this text.

Calculators

The use of calculators is essential in accounting. As the price of calculators continues to decrease, virtually every accounting employee will have a calculator available. Accounting students should be allowed to use this business tool, as calculators save time and increase accuracy. The use of calculators allows students to concentrate on the interpretation of a mathematical calculation rather than on the calculation itself. If possible, extra calculators should be available in the accounting classroom, for use by all students. Preferably, some of the calculators should be equipped with paper tape, which makes it possible for students to double check the figures being calculated.

SOURCES FOR HELP IN TEACHING ACCOUNTING

Accounting instructors have many outside sources of help available. Contact with one source typically leads to more sources, more ideas, and more information. Establishing and maintaining a network of resources should be a priority of all accounting instructors.

Publishing Companies

Representatives of accounting textbook publishing companies are an excellent resource for accounting instructors. Because these representatives are in contact with hundreds of other instructors, they can advise the instructor on methods and activities that have been effective in the accounting classroom. Company representatives are also a major source of information regarding new educational materials.

Professional Business Teacher Associations

Business educators are eligible to join any of several professional business teacher associations on the national, regional, and state level. These organizations publish educational materials, sponsor workshops and conventions, and support legislative and public relations efforts on behalf of business education. Membership allows educators to participate in conventions and workshops and to help develop the goals and objectives of the organizations. In addition, membership provides contact with other business educators throughout the country. Networking with other business educators is probably the best source of ideas and information available to any accounting instructor.

National Business Education Association. Organized at the national level, the National Business Education Association (NBEA) is a professional organization of business educators. In addition to publishing educational materials and curriculum guides and sponsoring conventions, NBEA publishes a monthly journal, *Business Education Forum*. NBEA is divided into five regional associations, which are further divided into state organizations.

Membership in NBEA includes membership in the regional association. Membership in the affiliated state association is handled by each state. For more information about NBEA, contact: NBEA Membership Director, 1914 Association Drive, Reston, Virginia 22091. Information about regional and state affiliates of NBEA can be obtained through NBEA.

Delta Pi Epsilon. Established to promote sound research in business education, Delta Pi Epsilon is a national organization with chapters at colleges and universities throughout the nation. Delta Pi Epsilon sponsors research, publishes a quarterly journal, sponsors workshops, and hosts a bi-annual national research conference. In addition, Delta Pi Epsilon publishes a yearly index of the major business education publications. Local chapters publish educational materials and sponsor meetings and workshops. More information can be obtained by contacting Delta Pi Epsilon National Office, P.O. Box 4340, Little Rock, Arkansas 72214.

Department of Education

The United States Department of Education is also a good source of general educational materials. Pamphlets, booklets, and books addressing a variety of educational topics are available by contacting the Superintendent of Documents, U.S. Government Printing Office, Washington, DC 20402.

Most states also have a Department of Education which can assist business educators. Many state departments publish curriculum materials, sponsor workshops and seminars, and provide information regarding contact persons (specialists and/or supervisors) in specific curriculum areas.

Local Specialists

Many local school districts (and states) have full-time business educational specialists. These specialists can be especially helpful in determining program or course content. Typically, specialists are aware of exemplary programs and courses within the state or district and can direct an instructor to other sources of help.

Professional Accountants Associations

Accounting instructors can also use the resources of professional accountants associations. These organizations provide career information about accounting and accounting-related fields, employment forecasts, and educational materials. More importantly, however, professional accountants associations can direct the accounting instructor to individuals who are willing to participate in shadowing experiences, serve as guest speakers or mentors, or host a field trip. Members of professional accountants associations are also excellent candidates for advisory committees.

Three major associations can be contacted at the following addresses:

American Institute of Certified Public Accountants, 1455 Pennsylvania Avenue N.W., Washington, DC 20004.

National Society of Public Accountants, 1010 N. Fairfax Street, Alexandria, Virginia 22314.

American Society of Women Accountants, 35 East Wacker Drive, Suite 1086, Chicago, Illinois 60601.

Advisory Committee

An advisory committee composed of local business persons and college representatives can be beneficial to an accounting program. This committee should include representatives from businesses which typically employ high school graduates, as well as accountants and those knowledgeable about accounting as a career. Including a local college accounting professor or department chairperson on the advisory committee is also beneficial. An advisory committee can be helpful in establishing minimum employment standards, reviewing course content, making recommendations to the administration concerning material and equipment needs, and establishing guidelines for articulation with post-secondary institutions. Members of the committee can also serve as a source of realistic accounting forms or other materials for the classroom.

Finally, advisory committee members may be willing to participate in shadowing experiences, serve as guest speakers or mentors, or host field trips.

Service Organizations

Local service organizations, such as the Chamber of Commerce, Rotary, Lions Club, and Kiwanis often have education committees whose members are willing to participate in shadowing experiences, serve as guest speakers or mentors, or host field trips.

Professional Journals and Publications

Many of the associations listed above publish journals or other materials which can be of assistance to the accounting instructor. Depending on the publisher, these materials may address educational issues or issues being discussed in the accounting field. The materials may be directed specifically at accounting education or address general education topics. All of these areas impact the accounting curriculum and should, therefore, be included in the professional readings of accounting instructors.

Electronic Bulletin Boards

The increasing use of computers in the home and school has resulted in the establishment of many electronic bulletin boards. Professional groups may fund or support electronic bulletin boards for their members. In addition, some state departments of education have state-sponsored electronic boards, with special conferences for business education.

OTHER CONSIDERATIONS

The accounting instructor should constantly be looking for new ideas, materials, procedures, and resources to incorporate into the teaching of accounting. Students, parents, or colleagues (or the spouse of a colleague) may have ideas or materials that will benefit the learning process.

In addition, bringing the public into the accounting classroom will enhance the credibility of the program. Members of various minority groups can serve as positive role models for minority students. Physically disabled persons holding accounting or accounting-related positions allow students to understand that varied opportunities in the field of accounting are available for everyone, regardless of disability.

CHAPTER 3
TEACHING TRANSACTION ANALYSIS

Transaction analysis is a thought process for dividing an accounting transaction into its debit and credit parts. Transaction analysis is used to accurately record all financial business activities. Only if these activities are recorded accurately can trust be placed in the financial statements produced at the end of an accounting period. Without the knowledge of an accurate method of transaction analysis, students will not understand the reasoning behind the action of debiting and crediting accounts.

ESSENTIAL ELEMENTS OF TRANSACTION ANALYSIS

The following activities comprise the elements which are essential to the understanding of transaction analysis.

Classifying Financial Data In The Basic Accounting Equation

The accounting equation is the foundation of double-entry accounting and is the basis for all future accounting knowledge. The accounting equation is used to understand how to increase and decrease account balances and to analyze transactions.

Learning Outcomes. Students must be able to accurately classify financial data within the elements of the accounting equation. The elements are (1) what the business owns (assets), (2) what the business owes (liabilities), and (3) what a business is worth (owner's equity).

Teaching Methods. In order to understand the accounting equation, students must learn the definition of each element in the equation as well as the relationship among the elements of the equation. Both goals can be developed simultaneously. The basic accounting equation builds on two elements.

> Items owned = Financial rights to items owned

With student input, list items owned by the school, a business, and/or an individual. Clarify the meaning of "financial rights to the items owned" as the right of an individual or a business to claim the assets of the business if the business were to declare bankruptcy or not pay its bills.

Since another term for "items owned" is "assets" and another term for "financial rights" is "equity," the second version of the equation is:

Assets = Equities

The following diagram is useful in helping students visualize this equation. Stress that the two sides are "in balance" as if on a balance-type scale.

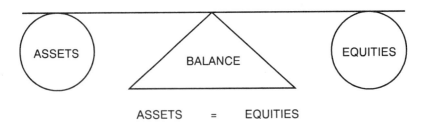

The discussion can then be focused on the two types of equities: (1) equity of those individuals or businesses to whom money is owed, and (2) equity of the owner(s). Have students list those businesses and/or individuals to whom the school, a business, and/or an individual owes money.

Once these dollar amounts are listed, stress that the two types of equities are separated into two categories. These categories are "liabilities" and "owner's equity." Therefore, the equation becomes:

Assets = Liabilities + Owner's Equity

The diagram can be changed as follows to show the two kinds of equities. Again, emphasize that the two sides are still "in balance."

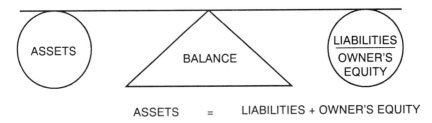

Once these terms are understood, focus the discussion on how to calculate the dollar amount of owner's equity and what that amount represents. Students and instructor, collectively, should list the assets and liabilities of the school in dollar amounts. Once the dollar amounts are listed, demonstrate the calculation of owner's equity as:

Assets − Liabilities = Owner's Equity

After plugging the amount of owner's equity into the original equation (assets = liabilities + owner's equity), explain the logic behind the equation using the school's list of assets, liabilities, and owner's equity. Students need to understand *why* assets equal the sum of the liabilities and owner's equity. The "financial rights" to the assets are divided between the rights of those to whom we owe money (liabilities) and the rights of the owners (owner's equity). Therefore, the sum of the liabilities and owner's equity *must* equal the total assets.

During the above discussions, the topic of several accounting concepts may be raised. These concepts include historic cost and unit of measurement. If these questions are raised by students, explain that there are accounting "rules" or concepts to follow and briefly explain the appropriate concept. Detailed discussion of accounting concepts should be delayed until a more appropriate time in the learning of the accounting cycle.

A suggested homework assignment is to have each student list personal assets and liabilities. Students should then calculate personal "owner's equity." Additional drills on classifying assets, liabilities, and owner's equity should also be completed individually by students.

Analyzing The Effects Of Transactions On The Accounting Equation

Each transaction affects at least two elements of the accounting equation. Business transactions can affect one or both sides of the accounting equation, but the equation must remain in balance after the transaction is recorded.

Learning Outcomes. Students must be able to correctly analyze the effects of transactions on the accounting equation. After recording the effect of a transaction, students must be able to prove the equality of the accounting equation.

Teaching Methods. After students understand the basic accounting equation, the next step is to discuss how the financial events of the business—the transactions—affect the equation. In order to build on previous learning, refer to the equations calculated in previous lessons (either the school's equation or the students' individual equations).

Ask if these equations have remained the same since the previous lesson or if the equation could have changed. The desired answer is that the equations could have changed. If the school bought an asset and promised to pay for it in the future, the school's equation would have changed. If any student spent money since completing a personal equation, that equation would have changed. Discussing these changes makes for a natural bridge to the topic of analyzing the effects of transactions on the accounting equation.

When actually analyzing the effects of transactions on the equation, start out with a new business, showing the original investment by the owner as the first transaction. The following diagram can be used to help set up a logical method of analyzing business transactions and may be developed either on a chalkboard or by the use of a progressive transparency. In addition, use confirmation as much as possible, asking questions rather than giving all important information in lecture format. Call on students to record the changes on the transparency or chalkboard or give each student a copy of the form to complete along with the instructor.

ASSETS			=	LIABILITIES	+	OWNER'S EQUITY
Cash	Supplies	Johnson Company	=	Smith Company		John Doe, Capital

Stress that the left side of the equation equals the right side of the equation. This statement needs to be repeated after every transaction is analyzed. In addition, explain that just like "Cash" is used to record the amount of money the business owns, "Capital" is used to record the amount of the owner's equity in the business.

Using this diagram, illustrate the effect that a $1,000.00 investment by the owner would have on the accounting equation. The transaction would increase the asset account, Cash, and would increase the owner's equity account, John Doe, Capital. After these changes have been determined, incorporate the changes into the diagram.

ASSETS			=	LIABILITIES	+	OWNER'S EQUITY
Cash	Supplies	Johnson Company	=	Smith Company		John Doe, Capital
+$1,000			=			+$1,000 (Investment)

The word "Investment" should be added near the capital account amount. This procedure will be helpful in the future when revenue and expenses are also listed under the capital column. Point out that both sides of the equation increased by $1,000; therefore, the equation is still in balance after the transaction has been recorded.

The second transaction could be that the business paid $50.00 cash for supplies. This transaction would decrease the asset account, Cash, and increase the asset account, Supplies. After these changes have been determined, incorporate the changes into the diagram.

ASSETS			=	LIABILITIES	+	OWNER'S EQUITY
Cash	Supplies	Johnson Company	=	Smith Company		John Doe, Capital
$1,000			=			$1,000 (Investment)
− 50	+50					
$ 950	$50		=			$1,000

Indicate that only one side of the equation changed because of the transaction; however, that side increased and decreased by the same amount. Therefore, the equation is still in balance after the transaction has been recorded.

Similar drills should be repeated several times. Make sure that all types of transactions affecting these accounts are covered. Students should be comfortable with this type of transaction before moving on to revenue and expense transactions.

When illustrating revenue and expense transactions, include the reason for the change in capital next to the amount of the change. For example, assume the business sold services for $100.00 on account to Johnson Company. The asset account, Johnson Company, and the owner's equity account, Capital, would both be increased. After these changes have been determined, incorporate the changes into the diagram.

ASSETS			=	LIABILITIES	+	OWNER'S EQUITY
Cash	Supplies	Johnson Company	=	Smith Company		John Doe, Capital
$1,000 −50	+50		=			$1,000 (Investment)
$ 950	$50	+100	=			$1,000 + 100 (Revenue)
$ 950	$50	$100	=			$1,100

As above, stress that both sides of the equation increased by equal amounts; therefore, the equation is still in balance after the transaction has been recorded. By differentiating between investment, revenue, and expense transactions, the instructor is leading into the idea of separating these transactions into individual accounts. This method also helps students understand how revenue and expense transactions affect owner's equity.

If the business paid $200 for utilities, the asset account, Cash, would decrease. The owner's equity account, Capital, would also decrease. After these changes have been determined, incorporate the changes into the diagram.

ASSETS			=	LIABILITIES	+	OWNER'S EQUITY
Cash	Supplies	Johnson Company	=	Smith Company		John Doe, Capital
$1,000 −50	+50		=			$1,000 (Investment)
$ 950	$50	+100	=			$1,000 + 100 (Revenue)
$ 950 −200	$50	$100	=			$1,100 −200 (Util. Exp.)
$750	$50	$100	=			$ 900

Both sides of the equation have decreased by equal amounts so the equation is still in balance after the transaction has been recorded.

Students should now be ready to attempt this analysis without instructor guidance. Numerous transactions should be assigned for individual practice. Students must be able to correctly analyze the effect of transactions on the accounting equation before moving on to the next topic. Move around the room as students are completing these drills, assisting students who need additional help and reinforcing correct answers.

Identifying Normal Account Balances, Increases And Decreases

Debit and credit theory rules govern the recording of increases and decreases in each type of account. The increase side of each account is also its normal balance side. Debit/credit theory is used to analyze transactions and as the basis for several accounting principles and procedures. The effect of debiting or crediting an account is important in order to understand transaction analysis, journalizing, posting, and the financial statements.

Learning Outcomes. Students must be able to identify the normal balance side, the increase side and the decrease side of accounts in the accounting equation. In addition, students must understand *why* the account increases or decreases on each side and how this procedure is used to keep the financial records of a business. Finally, students must understand what the balance of an account represents and how an account balance is used by the business.

Teaching Methods. In preparation for this next topic, explain that even though the equation has been useful to analyze the effects of transactions on the accounting equation, this format is not practical in daily business. A business with many different accounts would have an equation so long that it would be difficult to use efficiently. Therefore, a device called a "T account" is used. Draw a T account on the overhead or chalkboard and explain that the T account is a device used to analyze transactions. Point out that each account has a left side and a right side as illustrated.

left side	right side

Next, explain that in accounting, these are *not* referred to as "left side" and "right side," but are called the "debit side" and the "credit side."

left side	right side
DEBIT	CREDIT

Since students often have preconceived notions about the meaning of these terms (especially "credit"), stress that debit only means "left" and credit only means "right." Debits and credits are *not* good or bad but simply refer to the two sides of an account. Next, explain that each side is used to increase or decrease the account. Some accounts increase on the debit side and some increase on the credit side. However, an easy way to remember which side is used to increase or decrease each account is to relate each account back to the accounting equation.

Draw the following diagram on the overhead or chalkboard:

ASSETS	=	LIABILITIES	+	OWNER'S EQUITY
Asset		Liability		Owner's Capital

Debit	Credit	Debit	Credit	Debit	Credit

Explain that since assets are on the left side of the equation, assets increase on the left (or *debit*) side of the account. This means that if the transaction causes an asset account to increase, the amount of the increase would be recorded on the debit side of the asset account. In all cases, an account decreases on the side opposite its increase side; therefore, decreases to asset accounts are recorded on the *credit* side of the account. The diagram should be changed to:

ASSETS		=	LIABILITIES		+	OWNER'S EQUITY	
Asset			Liability			Owner's Capital	
Debit	Credit		Debit	Credit		Debit	Credit
Increases (+)	Decreases (−)						

Identical reasoning can be used to determine which side is used to record an increase and which side is used to record a decrease in liability accounts. Since liabilities are on the right side of the equation, liabilities increase on the right (or *credit*) side of the account. Therefore, if the transaction causes a liability account to increase, the amount of the increase would be recorded on the credit side of the liability account. All accounts decrease on the side opposite its increase side; therefore, decreases to liability accounts are recorded on the *debit* side of the account. The diagram should be changed to:

ASSETS		=	LIABILITIES		+	OWNER'S EQUITY	
Asset			Liability			Owner's Capital	
Debit	Credit		Debit	Credit		Debit	Credit
Increases (+)	Decreases (−)		Decreases (−)	Increases (+)			

Finally, use the same reasoning to explain which side is used to record an increase and which side is used to record a decrease in the owner's capital account. The diagram should be changed to:

ASSETS		=	LIABILITIES		+	OWNER'S EQUITY	
Asset			Liability			Owner's Capital	
Debit	Credit		Debit	Credit		Debit	Credit
Increases (+)	Decreases (−)		Decreases (−)	Increases (+)		Decreases (−)	Increases (+)

Before discussing changes in the revenue and expense accounts, the balance side of each type of account should be identified. Explain that the normal balance side of each account is the same as the increase side. Therefore, the diagram should be changed to:

ASSETS	=	LIABILITIES	+	OWNER'S EQUITY

Asset		Liability		Owner's Capital	
Debit	Credit	Debit	Credit	Debit	Credit
Increases (+)	Decreases (−)	Decreases (−)	Increases (+)	Decreases (−)	Increases (+)
Balance			Balance		Balance

Students must understand what is meant by the term "normal account balance." Demonstrate that in the Cash account, increases would be recorded on the debit side, decreases would be recorded on the credit side, and that when a balance is calculated, the account should have a debit balance.

```
              CASH
        $5,000  |  $1,500
         3,500  |   4,000
        ─────── |
     Balance $3,000
```

This balance means that the business owns $3,000 cash. Question students as to what the debit balance indicates in other asset accounts such as supplies, accounts receivable, prepaid insurance, etc. Also ask what a credit balance in an accounts receivable account would indicate. Use the same methods to discuss the "normal account balance" for liabilities and the owner's capital account. This discussion will help students understand what the balance of an account represents and how an account balance is used by the business.

In order to ensure that students can identify the normal account balance and the increase and decrease side for each of the three types of accounts, the instructor may want to prepare flash cards for drill on this topic. As more learning occurs, these flash cards can be expanded to include revenue and expense accounts.

To prepare the flash card, write the account title on the front of a card and the account title, classification, normal balance, increase side, and decrease side on the back of the card. As the front of the card is shown to the class, the instructor can tell from the back of the card which account is being considered. Flash the cards and ask students to respond to a question about the account. The best drill concentrates on going through the pack repeating the same question for each card. As students show evidence of having mastered the knowledge about a specific account title, remove that card from the pack.

The flash cards can also be used for short quizzes. Select ten account titles from the pack and arrange the cards in random order. Ask students to write on an answer sheet the account classification, the balance side, the increase side, or the decrease side.

The increases and decreases in other owner's equity accounts should be discussed in relation to the owner's capital account. The diagram on page 39 could be developed on the overhead or the chalkboard as the instructor leads the following discussion.

OWNER'S CAPITAL ACCOUNT	
Decrease	Increase

EXPENSES	
Increase	Decrease
Balance	

REVENUES	
Decrease	Increase
	Balance

DRAWING	
Increase	Decrease
Balance	

Revenue Accounts. Revenues increase the owner's capital. As previously discussed, capital increases on the credit side; therefore, increases in revenue accounts are recorded on the credit side of the revenue account. Decreases in revenue accounts are recorded on the debit side of the revenue account. Finally, revenue accounts normally have a credit balance.

Expense Accounts. Expenses decrease the owner's capital. As previously discussed, capital decreases on the debit side; therefore, increases in expense accounts are recorded on the debit side of the expense account. Decreases in expense accounts are recorded on the credit side of the expense account. Finally, expense accounts normally have a debit balance.

Drawing Account. The drawing account is used to record withdrawals by the owner(s). Withdrawals decrease the owner's capital, which decreases on the debit side. Therefore, increases in drawing are recorded on the debit side of the drawing account and decreases are recorded on the credit side of the drawing account. Finally, the drawing account normally has a debit balance.

As before, students must thoroughly understand how the process of debiting and/or crediting an account actually increases or decreases the balance of that account. Students also need to understand what the balance of a revenue, an expense, or the drawing account represents and how the business will use account balance information. As was previously suggested, the instructor could use flash cards to drill students on all of the above information. The account analysis summary in Illustration 3-1 can be duplicated and distributed to each student to be used as a study aid.

Analyzing Transactions Into Debit and Credit Parts

Each business transaction must be analyzed into debit and credit components. The accurate analysis of every transaction is essential to the integrity of the financial records of a business.

Learning Outcomes. Students must be able to correctly analyze transactions into debit and credit parts. To do this, students must combine the knowledge of (1) classifying financial data, (2) recognizing how transactions affect the equation, and (3) debit/credit theory and then apply this knowledge to the current transaction.

ACCOUNT ANALYSIS

TYPE OF ACCOUNT	INCREASE	DECREASE	NORMAL BALANCE
Asset	Debit	Credit	Debit
Liability	Credit	Debit	Credit
Capital	Credit	Debit	Credit
Revenue	Credit	Debit	Credit
Expense	Debit	Credit	Debit
Drawing	Debit	Credit	Debit

Illustration 3-1 Summary of Account Analysis

Students must understand and be able to use a step-by-step approach to analyzing transactions.

Teaching Methods. Present a step-by-step approach which the student can follow to analyze transactions into debit and credit parts. One such approach is to ask four questions as follows:

1. What accounts are affected by the transaction?
2. How is each account classified?
3. How is each account balance changed?
4. How is each amount entered in the accounts?

Model this approach using several different transactions. T accounts should also be used during this modeling. An example follows:

TRANSACTION: Received cash from the owner, Joan Smith, as an investment in the business, $3,000.

Step 1. *What accounts are affected by the transaction?*
Cash and Joan Smith, Capital

Step 2. *How is each account classified?*
Cash is an asset account; Joan Smith, Capital is an owner's equity account

Step 3. *How is each account balance changed?*
Cash is increased; Joan Smith, Capital is increased

Step 4. *How is each amount entered in the accounts?*
The asset account, Cash, is increased by a debit.
The owner's equity account, Joan Smith, Capital, is increased by a credit.

CASH		JOAN SMITH, CAPITAL
$3,000		$3,000

Point out that (1) at least two accounts are affected by each transaction, and (2) debits must equal credits for each transaction. Students should be instructed to verify these two items after every transaction.

Continue demonstrating this procedure by analyzing several different types of transactions. This procedure serves two purposes: (1) students learn to analyze transactions into debit and credit parts; and (2) students learn a procedure which is used throughout the course to analyze transactions.

This approach can also be taught using a prepared form to emphasize the four steps with one form for each transaction. A transparency could also be made for demonstration purposes. Distribute copies of each form for students to complete along with the instructor. A sample form follows:

Transaction				
Received cash from the owner, Joan Smith, as an investment in the business, $3,000.				
Analysis				
Account Affected	Account Classification	Increase/ Decrease + or −	Amount	
			Debited	Credited

Ask students to analyze the transaction shown on the transparency. As students respond, write the information for the analysis on the form. When the analysis is completed, the transparency would appear as follows:

Teaching Transaction Anaylsis

Transaction
Received cash from the owner, Joan Smith, as an investment in the business, $3,000.

Analysis

Account Affected	Account Classification	Increase/ Decrease + or −	Amount Debited	Amount Credited
Cash	Asset	+	$3,000	
Joan Smith, Capital	Owner's Equity	+		$3,000

CASH		JOAN SMITH, CAPITAL	
$3,000			$3,000

This approach emphasizes the decisions which have to be made about titles of accounts affected, the classification of each account, the increase or decrease caused by the transaction, and the way to record that change (debit or credit). A quick check of the Amount Debited and Credited columns helps students determine that debits equal credits in the analysis.

The T accounts at the bottom of the transparency help students visualize the analysis so that, after some practice, they can make the decisions mentally and enter the results directly in T accounts.

Since T accounts will be used throughout the student's study of accounting, require students to use T accounts for every transaction analyzed.

GENERAL CONSIDERATIONS

The use of bulletin boards throughout these topics is encouraged. Topic examples include the accounting equation, the balance-type scale representation of the equation, debit/credit theory rules, and the four steps in analyzing a transaction. Since these topics are essential for future accounting knowledge, try to convey the information to all students by using a variety of teaching aids. Remember that students learn in different ways; therefore, the more options available to students, the more likely students will master the material.

Throughout all accounting instruction, students should learn the *why* as well as the *how* of accounting procedures and concepts. The instructor should constantly assess if the *why* behind the *how* is being covered and understood: Do students understand *why* assets equal liabilities plus owner's equity? Do students understand *why* the increase side of an account is the same as the normal balance side? Do students understand what the account balance represents? Do students understand *why* cash is debited when money is received?

Whenever possible, relate new information back to previous knowledge, especially tying it back to the basic accounting equation. In this way, students will be able to think problems through logically and will be more likely to see the relationships involved.

Explain that transaction analysis is the cornerstone of accurate accounting. Encourage students to follow the step-by-step method for analyzing transactions into debit and credit parts by using the steps for every transaction. Good modeling is an excellent way to demonstrate the importance of the step-by-step method and will encourage students to follow the same procedure when analyzing transactions into debit and credit parts without instructor guidance.

Students will gradually move from the step-by-step process to immediately "knowing" how to record the transaction in the appropriate accounts. This mastery of transaction analysis will come from extensive drill and practice using the procedures discussed in this chapter.

CHAPTER 4
TEACHING JOURNALS AND JOURNALIZING

A journal is often called "the book of original entry." Journals serve three major purposes: (1) they provide a permanent, chronological listing of the activities of the business; (2) they serve as a quick check of the equality of debits and credits for each transaction; and (3) they supply the total picture of each transaction in one location. A journal may be thought of as a business diary showing the sequence of financial events of a business.

Many different types of journals are used in business. Although the name and the type of journal varies from one business to another, all businesses use some form of journal device to record business transactions. Since graduating high school accounting students often obtain entry-level accounting jobs, which include a high proportion of activity in the recording functions, a mastery of journals and journalizing is necessary.

ESSENTIAL ELEMENTS OF JOURNALS AND JOURNALIZING

Journalizing is included in various chapters and topics throughout an accounting course, rather than being isolated in a single chapter. The following activities comprise the elements which are essential to the understanding of journals and journalizing.

Recognizing The Common Features Of Journals

All journals have certain features in common, such as (1) a Date column, (2) an Account Title column, and (3) a Posting Reference column. Many, but not all, journals have other features in common, such as (1) a Document Number column, (2) General Debit and/or General Credit amount columns, and (3) special amount columns.

Learning Outcomes. Students must be able to recognize the common features of journals. Students must also understand *why* businesses use different journals and how a business decides which journal(s) to use.

Teaching Methods. When a new journal is presented, identify the features the new journal has in common with previously learned journals and drill students on the use of the common columns. After this review, concentrate on the new learning related to the journal.

Journals are designed to meet the needs of the business. The business must analyze the number and types of transactions in which it is normally involved and determine which journals and which special columns are needed to most efficiently record daily transactions.

Bulletin board displays can highlight the common features of the journals to be studied.

Journalizing Transactions In A General Journal

A general journal contains two amount columns. All transactions can be recorded in a general journal.

Learning Outcomes. Students must be able to accurately journalize transactions in a general journal, using correct form. This includes recording the date of the entry, the debit part of the entry, the credit part of the entry, and (in some journals) the explanation for the entry. Students must also know how to prove the equality of the debit and credit amounts recorded in the entry.

Teaching Methods. When a special journals approach is used, students are usually first introduced to a two-column general journal similar to the journal in Illustration 4–1.

GENERAL JOURNAL   Page _____

Date	Account Title	Doc. No.	Post. Ref.	Debit	Credit

Illustration 4–1 Two-column General Journal

Remind students that all transactions should be <u>thoroughly analyzed *before*</u> the <u>transaction is journalized</u>. Once the analysis is complete, students can begin to record the journal entry. Guide students through the first few entries. Illustrate the entry on the chalkboard or on a transparency, while students individually complete the same entry on journal paper.

A correct general journal entry includes several items entered in correct form. Stress the guidelines for entering the date of the entry. Correct placement of the account titles is also important. The Doc. No. column is used to record the number of the source document, establishing an "audit trail" which provides a means of tracking the information to the original source if subsequent verification of the entry is needed. If this column is included in the two-column general journal, no explanation line is required.

Note: If the general journal does not have a Doc. No. column, a short explanation is given as the last line of the entry. This explanation includes the number of the source document which supports the entry.

After completing several journal entries together, give students a series of journal entries to be completed on an individual basis.

Journalizing Transactions In Multi-Column Journals

A business may choose to use a multi-column journal instead of the general journal. A multi-column journal contains special amount columns to be used for frequently occurring transactions.

Simple Multi-Column Journal. The first multi-column journal introduced should be a simple one with a minimum of special amount columns.

1. Learning Outcomes. Students must be able to accurately journalize transactions in a simple multi-column journal. Accurate journalizing includes knowing when, why, and how to use the general amount columns and the special amount columns; when to write in the account title; and how to prove the equality of the debit and credit amounts recorded in the entry.

2. Teaching Methods. If the general journal has already been introduced, previous knowledge should be used as a foundation to introduce the simple multi-column journal. Illustrate the general journal on a transparency or the chalkboard. A quick review of this journal can be accomplished by journalizing the following entry:

TRANSACTION: Sept. 1 Received cash from the owner, John Doe, as an investment, $1,000.00, Receipt No. 1.

While students describe the entry, record the information on the transparency or chalkboard. Next, display a simple multi-column journal, similar to Illustration 4–2, on a transparency or the chalkboard.

JOURNAL   Page _____

Date	Account Title	Doc. No.	Post. Ref.	General		Sales	Cash	
				Debit	Credit	Credit	Debit	Credit

Illustration 4–2   Five-column Multi-column Journal

Comment that a multi-column journal is created when special amount columns are added to a two-column general journal. The most common special columns are for cash and sales transactions. Describe why the special columns are used and demonstrate how to record the debit to Cash, $1,000.00, for the September 1 entry. Ask students to recall previous learning and describe how to record the remainder of the entry.

If the five-column journal is the first journal students learn, point out the columns that are common to all journals (Date, Account Title, Post. Ref.) and describe why special columns are used. Remind students that all transactions should be thoroughly analyzed *before* the transaction is journalized. Once the analysis is complete, students can begin to record the journal entry. Students should be guided through the first few entries. Illustrate the entry on the chalkboard or on a transparency, while students complete the same entry on journal paper.

A correct multi-column journal entry includes several items entered in correct form. Stress the guidelines for entering the date of the entry. Correct usage of special and general amount columns is also important. Students need to understand when to write an account title in the Account Title column and when the account title is not necessary. The Doc. No. column is used to record the number of the source document in order to establish an "audit trail." An audit trail provides a means of tracking the information to the original source if subsequent verification of the entry is needed.

Whether students have previously used a general journal or not, this first explanation about using a special amount column is important. The same rules are used for all other special amount columns regardless of the journal in which they occur. Therefore, the instructor should stress four guidelines regarding the use of special amount columns.

1. *Why special amount columns are used in journals.* A special amount column is used for each account for which many entries are made each month. Special amount columns require less space and less lines when recording and posting entries.

2. *How to recognize a special amount column.* An account title, such as Cash Debit, appears in the heading of a special amount column.

3. *How to decide when to record an amount in a special amount column.* If the debit or credit part of an entry is the same as a column heading, the amount is recorded in that special amount column. For example, if the transaction analysis shows that Cash should be debited and there is a Cash Debit column, the amount is recorded in that column and the account title, Cash, does not need to be written in the Account Title column.

4. *How to record an account title for an account.* Students must know two things about recording account titles in journals. (a) If an amount is recorded in a GENERAL amount column, the related general ledger account title *is* recorded in the Account Title column. (b) If an amount is recorded in a SPECIAL amount column, the related general ledger account title *is not* recorded in the Account Title column because the title is in the column heading.

Next, illustrate a transaction that only uses special amount columns.

TRANSACTION: Sept. 3 Received cash from sales, $500.00, Tape No. 1.

Students should analyze the transaction and determine which accounts to debit and credit. Ask students to describe how to record the debit to Cash and the credit to Sales in the journal. As students respond, record the entry on the transparency or chalkboard.

After both amounts have been entered in special amount columns, describe how a check mark is placed in the Account Title column to show that no account title needs to be written there. All relevant account titles are in special amount column headings. Also explain that a check mark is placed in the Post. Ref. column to show that no separate amounts are posted from this line and mention that posting from the journal will be covered later. (Posting from special amount columns will be described in Chapter 5 of this text.)

After the demonstration and class discussion, students should be given a series of transactions with which they have already worked. Have students analyze and record the transaction in a multi-column journal. When this drill has been completed, assign one or two additional problems in which students will (1) analyze transactions using T accounts and (2) record the transactions in a simple multi-column journal.

A bulletin board could be prepared summarizing the evolution from the two-column general journal to the simple multi-column journal. The bulletin board, Illustration 4–3, should be expanded as each new journal is presented to continue showing the evolution process and emphasizing the common features of all journals.

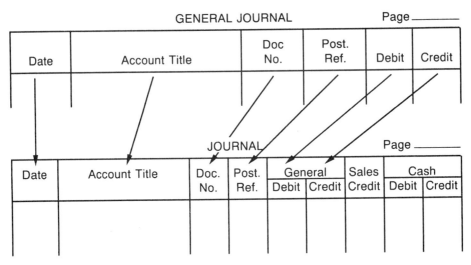

Illustration 4–3 Bulletin Board Showing the Evolution of Journals

The bulletin board can be altered to illustrate the evolution of any series of journals, thereby customizing it to match the journal approach used in the course.

Expanded Multi-Column Journal. The expanded multi-column journal (or combination journal) is a simple multi-column journal with additional special amount columns.

1. Learning Outcomes. Students must be able to accurately journalize transactions in an expanded multi-column journal, including knowing how and when to use the additional special amount columns.

2. Teaching Methods. The procedure for introducing the expanded multi-column journal is similar to that used for moving from a general journal to a simple multi-column journal. Begin the lesson by asking students to describe an entry in the journal that students know. Next, illustrate the new journal on a transparency or the chalkboard. The new special columns should be pointed out. Ask students to discuss why the new columns have been added to the journal. The expanded multi-column journal is similar to Illustration 4–4.

Page _____   JOURNAL

Date	Account Title	Doc. No.	Post. Ref.	General Debit	General Credit	Accounts Receivable Debit	Accounts Receivable Credit

(left-hand page)

Page _____

Sales Credit	Sales Tax Payable Credit	Accounts Payable Debit	Accounts Payable Credit	Purchases Debit	Cash Debit	Cash Credit

(right-hand page)

Illustration 4–4   An Expanded Multi-column Journal

If the use of controlling accounts and subsidiary ledgers is studied at the same time the expanded multi-column journal is introduced, additional information must be added to the four guidelines on page 47. Guideline 4 should be expanded by adding: (c) If an amount *is* recorded in a SPECIAL amount column headed with the name of a general ledger controlling account, the affected subsidiary ledger account title *is* written in the Account Title column. Demonstrate an entry by asking students to analyze a payment on account transaction. Describe and illustrate how to record the transaction in the journal and explain why the subsidiary ledger account title is written in the Account Title column. Students should complete additional drills involving subsidiary ledger accounts.

If the use of controlling accounts and subsidiary ledgers is *not* studied at the same time the expanded multi-column journal is introduced, explain that the name of the business needs to be written in the Account Title column. Illustrate how to write the name in the Account Title column. Finally, mention that the reason for this will be explained in more detail in future chapters.

The bulletin board described on page 48 can be expanded to show the continued evolution of the journals used in the course.

Journalizing Transactions In Special Journals

A business with many daily transactions may choose to use a separate journal for each kind of transaction. A journal used to record only one kind of transaction is referred to as a special journal.

Learning Outcomes. Students must be able to accurately journalize transactions in special journals. If students have previously worked with special amount columns, new learning consists of recognizing a special journal, knowing why special journals are used, determining which special journal to use, and transferring existing knowledge and skills to the special journal.

If students have not previously worked with multi-column journals, this will be students' first exposure to special amount columns. Therefore, in addition to the above skills, students must also know when, why, and how to use the general amount columns or the special amount columns; when the account title is necessary; and how to prove the equality of the debit and credit amounts recorded in the entry.

Teaching Methods. If students have previously worked with special amount columns, project a transparency of a special journal and ask students to determine the common features of the journal. Students should identify which columns have been used in other journals studied. Stress that very little new learning is necessary to make an entry in a special journal. New columns, such as Purchase Discount Credit, Check No., etc., need to be explained and discussed.

Introduce each special journal by having students record a specific entry in a multi-column journal. Next, record the entry in the appropriate special journal, pointing out the similarities and the differences in the two entries. By pointing out the similarities between the entries, students will benefit by transfer of previous knowledge.

Finally, drill students on which special journal should be used for each transaction in a series of transactions. Homework assignments should consist of drills to determine which special journal to use and problems which provide practice at recording entries in special journals.

If students have not previously worked with special amount columns, follow the same series of steps as described above for using simple multi-column journals substituting the special journal in place of the multi-column journal. In addition, controlling accounts and subsidiary ledgers need to be explained. Follow the suggestions given above regarding controlling accounts and subsidiary ledgers.

The bulletin board described above can be expanded to show the continued evolution of the journals used in the course.

Checking the Accuracy of Journals

Since the journal is the first place a transaction is recorded, it is the foundation of the accounting system. Accuracy is essential when making journal entries. An inaccurate journal entry will produce inaccurate financial statements.

Learning Outcomes. Students must be able to check the accuracy of journals. This accuracy check involves checking the equality of debits and credits for (1) each entry, and (2) the journal as a compete unit.

Teaching Methods. Regardless of the journal being used, students should immediately check to determine that the debit amount equals the credit amount for the entry just recorded. Stress the importance of the equality check by verifying for equality after *every* demonstration entry.

The equality of debits and credits for a complete journal (except the general journal) is checked by comparing the totals of the amount columns. If the journal has more than one amount column, the sum of the debit column totals must equal the sum of the credit column totals. Describe this procedure and use a completed journal for demonstration purposes. Students should total each amount column. Assuming students are using a multi-column journal, illustrate the procedure on the chalkboard or transparency, using the following format.

COLUMN	DEBIT COLUMN TOTAL	CREDIT COLUMN TOTAL
General	$ 500.00	$ 100.00
Sales		2,600.00
Cash	6,100.00	3,900.00
Totals	$6,600.00	$6,600.00

The same procedure is used for expanded multi-column journals and for all special journals with more than one amount column. Special journals with only one amount column are also checked for accuracy. An accuracy check is done by totaling the amount column and re-adding the column in reverse order. The accuracy of the general journal as a unit is not checked.

Checking the accuracy of journals as a complete unit is important. Convey the importance of this procedure by modeling the procedure after each journal is totaled.

Ruling Journals

Once a journal is totaled and the accuracy of the journal is proved, the journal is ruled.

Learning Outcomes. Students must be able to follow common procedures used to rule journals and to decide when to rule journals.

Teaching Methods. Ruling procedures are the same for all journals except the general journal, which is not totaled and, therefore, is not ruled. Stress the following guides for ruling a journal.

1. A single line is ruled across all amount columns to show that these columns are to be totaled.
2. On the next line, the last day of the month is written in the Date column.
3. The word "Total" is written in the Account Title column.
4. Column totals are written below the single line.
5. Double lines are ruled across all amount columns to indicate that the totals have been verified as correct.

Demonstrate the ruling procedure only on the first journal requiring ruling. As new journals requiring ruling are introduced, ask students to apply what they previously learned in ruling to the new journal. Model good ruling by always using a ruler and making neat, straight lines.

GENERAL CONSIDERATIONS

Journals are designed according to the needs of each business. Therefore, no two businesses are likely to use journals that are exactly the same.

Since journalizing is included in many chapters throughout an accounting course and journals are introduced in different combinations, student learning should be a building process. The features of the journal introduced first should be used to introduce the next journal. In that way, students can apply previous learning to each new journal studied.

Model good journalizing standards by using transparencies and/or the chalkboard to illustrate journal entries. Errors should be corrected by drawing a single line through the error and writing the correction above the error. Entries should be neat and in correct format, with lines straight and neat.

Finally, stress that no matter which journal is being used, the transaction should be fully analyzed before the entry is made in the appropriate journal.

CHAPTER 5
TEACHING LEDGERS AND POSTING

The ledgers of a business are the basis of its financial statements. The balances in the ledger accounts are used to prepare the financial statements, which are used to make important financial decisions relating to the business. If the financial statements are to accurately reflect the financial position of the business, the ledgers must be accurate. In order for the ledger accounts to be accurate, the postings to those accounts must be accurate.

In addition to making journal entries, entry level accounting positions also require posting to ledger accounts. High school accounting students need to master posting procedures as well as understand the functions of ledger forms.

Early in an accounting course, students learn how to post to a general ledger, while posting to subsidiary ledger accounts is presented later in the course. If students learn the correct procedure for posting the first time it is presented, previous knowledge can be applied to subsequent lessons relating to posting.

ESSENTIAL ELEMENTS OF LEDGERS AND POSTING

Ledgers and posting to ledgers are two topics which are included in numerous chapters throughout an accounting course, rather than being isolated in a single chapter. The following activities comprise the elements which are essential to the understanding of ledgers and posting.

Constructing A Chart Of Accounts

A listing of each account title and number is referred to as a chart of accounts. When setting up the chart of accounts for a business, common practices should be followed.

General Ledger. The general ledger is used by all businesses and is the first ledger that students will encounter in an accounting course.

1. Learning Outcomes. Students must be able to construct a general ledger chart of accounts according to ledger divisions, classify and list accounts in the divisions, and number the accounts.

2. Teaching Methods. Before learning how to construct a chart of accounts, students have already encountered the need for account titles. Students have used account titles to analyze transactions into debit and credit parts. Students may have, at some point, questioned what the title of an account should be. For example, students may have used the title Supplies when the instructor used the title Supplies—Office.

Remind students that account titles have been used and discussed throughout the process of analyzing transactions. Introduce the need for a business to have a list of all the account titles and numbers that will be used for financial reporting. Explain that the listing should be constructed in some kind of logical order and is commonly the same order in which it is listed on financial statements.

At this point, project a transparency of a skeleton outline of a chart of accounts similar to Illustration 5–1. Emphasize the general outline of the basic chart of accounts. Students should understand that the chart of accounts includes five divisions and that each division of the chart of accounts is numbered sequentially.

HELFRY COMPANY
CHART OF ACCOUNTS

(1) Assets	(4) Revenue
(2) Liabilities	(5) Expenses
(3) Owner's Equity	

Illustration 5-1 Skeleton Outline of a Chart of Accounts

Explain that the assets division is assigned the number 1, the liabilities division is assigned the number 2, etc. Drill students by calling out account titles. Students should respond with the division number for that account.

Next, explain that each account number begins with the division number for that account's classification. For example, the account number for the Cash account begins with the digit 1. Again, verbally drill students on the first digit of various accounts. The first time students work with a chart of accounts, the account numbers may consist of two or three digits. For illustrative purposes, this text will assume that students are immediately introduced to three-digit account numbers.

At this point, introduce the three-digit account number, explaining that the second two digits indicate the location of each account within a general ledger division. Furthermore, the accounts within each division should be listed in the order the accounts appear on financial statements; therefore, within the Asset division, Cash has a lower account number than Accounts Receivable. Discuss the possibility of skipping account numbers when the chart of accounts is originally constructed so that new accounts can be placed in the correct location within a division. For example, Cash may be assigned the number 110 Accounts Receivable, the number 120, and so on.

After the above discussion, give students a list of account titles, which should include accounts from the narrative of the textbook and accounts used during journalizing. The list should be in alphabetical order. The following is an example:

Advertising Expense	Petty Cash
Bailey Office Supplies (creditor)	Prepaid Insurance
Cash	Rent Expense
Davis Cleaning Supplies (creditor)	Repair Expense
Pat Hoyer, Capital	Sales
Pat Hoyer, Drawing	Supplies
Income Summary	Supplies Expense
Insurance Expense	Utilities Expense
Miscellaneous Expense	

Students should decide the placement and assign an account number for each account on the chart. As students respond, add each account title and number to the skeleton outline until the chart of accounts is complete.

Use caution when presenting the initial chart of accounts. Stress that account titles and the numbers assigned to the accounts are designed to fit the needs of the business. Since each business has varying needs, charts of accounts will also vary. Each division on the chart is not *always* given the same number used on the basic chart of accounts. For example, EXPENSES is not always the fifth division. In a subsequent accounting cycle a COST OF MERCHANDISE division is added. COST OF MERCHANDISE is then the fifth division and EXPENSES is the sixth division. In subsequent cycles, some of the divisions will be separated into subdivisions. For example, ASSETS will be divided into Current Assets and Plant Assets. Finally, account numbers may be larger than three digits.

As students study subsequent accounting cycles with expanded charts of accounts, new learning should be based on previous learning. To build on previous knowledge, begin with a chart of accounts students already know. Expand the chart of accounts to include new divisions, subdivisions, and/or new accounts.

As each new chart of accounts is discussed, give students a list of currently-used accounts. Students should be able to place each account in the correct division and assign it an appropriate account number.

Subsidiary Ledger. As the number of accounts in a general ledger increases because of a growth in business activities, the number of entries in the general ledger becomes too large to handle efficiently. Consequently, a business may group some common accounts together in a separate ledger. The accounts that have been removed from the general ledger are grouped together in what is referred to as a "subsidiary ledger." Common subsidiary ledgers include the Accounts Receivable Subsidiary Ledger and the Accounts Payable Subsidiary Ledger. The one account in the general ledger that summarizes all of the accounts in the subsidiary ledger is referred to as a "controlling" account.

1. Learning Outcomes. Students must understand why subsidiary ledgers are used, which accounts are typically placed in a subsidiary ledger, how to set up a subsidiary ledger, and the purpose of controlling accounts.

2. Teaching Methods. Explain the reason for subsidiary ledgers and how subsidiary ledgers help a business. To emphasize how subsidiary ledgers help a business, ask students to imagine the trial balance for a large, local retail department store. If each customer has an account in the general ledger, each customer's name will appear on the trial balance. Such a long trial balance can become quite a problem for the business. One solution is to take all similar accounts, such as all accounts receivable, and keep them separate from the general ledger. Stress, however, that if all accounts receivables are removed from the general ledger, the general ledger will not be in balance — debits will not equal credits. The solution is to have one account in the general ledger that will summarize all of the accounts receivable that have been removed from the general ledger.

Explain that businesses commonly set up subsidiary ledgers for accounts receivable and accounts payable.

Use the diagram in Illustration 5-2 to help students visualize the relationship between the general ledger and the subsidiary ledgers. Students should understand that no matter how many accounts are in the subsidiary ledger, only one controlling account is used to summarize each subsidiary ledger.

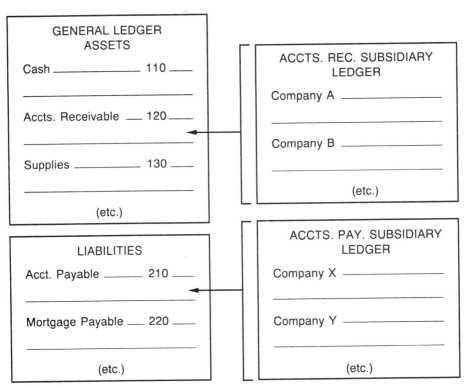

Illustration 5-2
Relationship Between the General Ledger and the Subsidiary Ledgers

Explain that a controlling account serves two purposes: (1) The account provides a place in the general ledger to summarize debits and credits to individual ledger accounts and helps maintain the equality of general ledger debits and credits. (2) The account provides an internal accuracy check in a subsidiary ledger because the balance of a controlling account must be the same as the sum of all subsidiary ledger account balances. Illustration 5-3 can be used to help students understand (2) above.

Finally, explain that since customers and vendors are constantly being added and removed from the records of a business, customers' and vendors' accounts are not assigned an account number in the subsidiary ledgers but are placed in alphabetical order in each ledger. Mention, however, that an exception may exist in automated accounting systems, where all accounts are assigned an account number.

Students need practice in setting up and arranging accounts in subsidiary ledgers. Give students a list of charge customers and ask them to correctly organize the

```
        GENERAL LEDGER                        ACCTS. REC. SUBSIDIARY
            ASSETS                                    LEDGER
   Cash _____ 110__           Company A _____
                                                          Bal. 350.00

   Accts. Receivable _____ 120__         Company B _____
               Balance                                    Bal. 750.00
          Dr.   |   Cr.
         1500.00|                        Company C _____
                                                          Bal. 400.00
```

Illustration 5–3
Balance in Control Account = Sum of Subsidiary Ledger Account Balance

accounts for an accounts receivable subsidiary ledger. A similar drill can be developed for vendors in an accounts payable subsidiary ledger.

The illustrations given above can be used as a transparency and/or a bulletin board to assist students in visualizing the relationship between the general ledger controlling account and the subsidiary ledger accounts.

Recognizing Which Items In Journals Need To Be Posted

Some individual amounts and some column totals must be posted from various journals. Although posting procedures vary with the journal, some posting procedures are the same for more than one journal.

Learning Outcomes. Students must be able to recognize which individual amounts and which column totals in a journal need to be posted. Students must be able to transfer knowledge of posting to all journals used in the accounting course.

Teaching Methods. Before students can post journal entries, they must be drilled on recognizing which amounts are to be posted. Display a transparency containing the following guides for posting:

1. Separate amounts recorded in any journal's general amount columns *are* posted individually to the account written in the Account Title column.
2. Totals of any journal's general amount columns *are not* posted.
3. Separate amounts recorded in any journal's special amount columns *are not* posted individually *unless* the special amount column heading is a controlling account for a subsidiary ledger. If the special amount column heading is a controlling account, individual amounts recorded in the column *are* posted separately to the subsidiary ledger account listed in the journal's Account Title column.
4. Totals of any journal's special amount columns *are* posted to the account named in the special amount column heading.

Teaching Ledgers and Posting

Discuss the posting guides and stress that the guides apply to *all* journals. As a reinforcement drill, display a transparency of each journal studied in the course up to this point. The journals should be totaled and ruled. Point to individual amounts or column totals and have individual students state if the amount is posted or not posted. After the drill, students should be able to complete individual practice drills requiring them to actually post journals with which they are familiar.

As a summary of the guides to posting, prepare a bulletin board showing the journal being studied and indicating whether or not individual amounts are posted separately and whether totals are posted. A bulletin board showing the posting guides for a simple multi-column journal is shown in Illustration 5-4. A similar bulletin board could be prepared for each journal as the journal is studied.

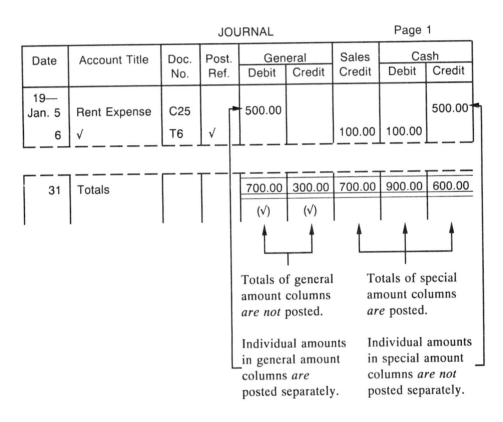

Illustration 5–4 Posting Guides for a Multi-column Journal

Posting From Journals To Ledgers

The actual transferring of information from a journal entry to a ledger account is referred to as posting. Posting updates the balance of each ledger account and must be completed before financial statements are prepared.

Learning Outcomes. Students must understand the importance of posting and why posting is done. In addition, students must be able to accurately transfer data from journals to general or subsidiary ledger accounts.

Teaching Methods. In order to introduce posting, display a completed journal page and review the benefits of using a journal (see Chapter 4). Ask if there are any disadvantages to *only* using a journal to record business transactions. The desired answer is that the balance in any account is not immediately known. In order to calculate the balance in the Cash account, for example, an employee would have to look through every journal entry for either debits or credits to Cash. Using these amounts, the balance in the Cash account could be calculated. This method of calculating account balances would be time-consuming and inaccurate.

Continue by explaining that copying (or posting) the information from the journal to individual ledger accounts gives the business the information it needs to operate.

Stress that *both* the journal entries and the posted ledger accounts are important financial records for the business.

Once the need for and the importance of posting has been discussed, inform students that posting procedures follow very specific rules and are completed in a very specific sequence. Following a specific sequence assures that all the posting work is completed accurately. Without close supervision during the early learning stages, students often develop their own posting procedures which seem easier or quicker. Care must be taken that initial posting practice is done in class, under the instructor's supervision, until students have fully learned and are using the correct procedure.

The first four steps in posting are the same regardless of which journal is being posted or whether posting an individual amount or a column total. Discuss and demonstrate the following posting steps. In order to illustrate both the journal page and the ledger accounts at the same time, prepare a completed journal on the chalkboard and display the accounts on a transparency.

1. Write the date of the entry in the Date column of the account.
2. Write the journal page number in the Post. Ref. column of the account.
3. Write the amount in the Debit or Credit column of the account.
4. Calculate the new account balance and write it in the Balance Debit or Credit column of the account.
5. (a) If posting an individual amount to a general ledger account, write the number of the account in the Post. Ref. column of the journal.
   (b) If posting an individual amount to a subsidiary ledger account, place a check mark in the Post. Ref. column of the journal.
   (c) If posting a total, write the number of the account in the amount column of the journal below the double rule.

Students should learn to perform the steps for posting in the sequence listed above. To reinforce the sequence, ask students to practice recalling the steps until they do so with ease. Caution students as to the danger involved in not following these steps in sequence. By following the steps, students will always know exactly how much of the entry has been posted. If interrupted, students can quickly determine which steps have been completed and continue posting from that point.

A bulletin board can be prepared illustrating the five posting steps. The design for such a bulletin board is given in Illustration 5–5.

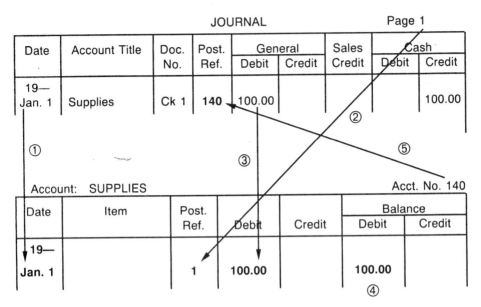

Illustration 5–5   Five Steps in Posting

GENERAL CONSIDERATIONS

Again, explain the *why* behind the topics presented in this chapter including *why* a business needs a chart of accounts, *why* a subsidiary ledger is helpful, *why* some amounts are posted individually and some are posted as totals, *why* the posting steps must be completed in order, and *why* posting is necessary.

If the general guidelines given in this chapter are emphasized, students will be able to apply these guidelines to similar accounting situations, whether in school or on the job.

CHAPTER **6**
TEACHING ANALYSIS OF ADJUSTMENTS AND THE WORK SHEET

Show how adjustments affect balance sheet and income statement

Generally accepted accounting practice requires that revenue from business activities and expenses associated with earning that revenue are recorded in the same accounting period. Recording all revenue and expenses for a fiscal period is generally referred to as the concept of matching expenses with revenue. In order to apply the matching concept, some general ledger accounts must be brought up to date (adjusted) at the end of a fiscal period before the financial statements are prepared.

ESSENTIAL ELEMENTS OF ADJUSTMENTS AND THE WORK SHEET

Adjusting entries and the work sheet are included in numerous chapters throughout an accounting course rather than being isolated in a single chapter. The following activities comprise the elements which are essential to the understanding of adjustments and the work sheet.

Recording a Trial Balance on a Work Sheet

A work sheet is a planning tool designed to assist in end-of-fiscal-period accounting work. Before beginning end-of-period work on a work sheet, equality of debits and credits is proved. The proof of debits and credits is referred to as a trial balance. Information for the trial balance is taken from the general ledger accounts.

Learning Outcomes. Students must be able to correctly transfer account titles and balances in the general ledger to the trial balance columns on a work sheet. In addition, students must be able to add all debit account balances, add all credit account balances, and verify that the sum of the debit account balances equals the sum of the credit account balances.

Teaching Methods. Prepare transparencies of a set of general ledger accounts as the accounts would appear at the end of the fiscal period. On the chalkboard, write the heading of a work sheet and explain that the work sheet is a planning tool for the accountant.

Write the first three columns of the work sheet—Account Title, Trial Balance Debit, and Trial Balance Credit—on the chalkboard. If this is the first time students have completed a trial balance, explain that the trial balance is a device used to determine if the accounts with debit balances equal the accounts with credit balances in the general ledger.

Complete the trial balance on the chalkboard following the seven steps listed below. Give a blank work sheet form to each student to complete as the demonstration progresses.

1. Write the general ledger account titles in the Account Title column of the work sheet. All accounts, even those with a zero balance, should be included.
2. Write the general ledger account debit balances in the Trial Balance Debit column. Write the general ledger account credit balances in the Trial Balance Credit column.
3. Rule a single line across the two Trial Balance columns below the last line on which an account title is written.
4. Add both the Trial Balance Debit and Credit columns.
5. Check the equality of the two amount column totals. If not equal, find the error, enter the corrected balance, re-add the Trial Balance Debit and Credit columns and again check the equality of the two amount column totals.
6. Write each column's total below the single line.
7. Rule double lines across both Trial Balance columns.

While completing the trial balance, call on individual students to provide information that should be written on each line of the trial balance. When all account titles and balances are written on the work sheet, have each student add the debit and credit columns of the trial balance. Call on several students to give their totals. Emphasize the importance of making sure the debit total equals the credit total before continuing.

A completed trial balance is given in Illustration 6–1.

Lopez Secretarial Service
Work Sheet
For Month Ended June 30, 19—

Account Title	Trial Balance	
	Debit	Credit
Cash	5,500.00	
Supplies	100.00	
Prepaid Insurance	600.00	
Buscher Paper Supply		500.00
Morse Janitorial Supplies		800.00
Martin Lopez, Capital		2,400.00
Martin Lopez, Drawing		700.00
Sales		2,200.00
Advertising Expense	300.00	
Insurance Expense		
Supplies Expense		
Utilities Expense	100.00	
	6,600.00	6,600.00

Illustration 6–1 Completed Trial Balance

Identifying the Accounts That Need to be Adjusted

At the end of an accounting period, some accounts have changed in value, but the changes have not been recorded in the accounts. Before adjusting entries can be made, accounts needing adjustment must be identified.

Learning Outcomes. Initially, students will be given the accounts that need to be adjusted for the accounting period. Eventually, however, students must be able to identify the accounts that need to be adjusted in order to do end-of-fiscal-period accounting work.

Teaching Methods. Identifying accounts that need to be adjusted is not taught as an isolated topic. Beginning accounting students would find it difficult to identify which accounts need adjusting without knowing what an adjusting entry is or what effect it has on the financial statements. Instead, incorporate the topic of identifying accounts that need to be adjusted into the lecture for *every* adjusting entry. Beginning with the very first discussion of adjusting entries, stress *why* the adjusting entry is done and what effect the entry has on the financial statements of the business. If students understand why adjusting entries are done, they will be able to identify the accounts that need adjusting.

Analyzing General Ledger Account Adjustments

Before an adjusting entry can be planned on a work sheet, each account adjustment must be analyzed into its debit and credit parts. Adjusting entries are introduced throughout an accounting course rather than being isolated in one chapter.

First Cycle—Prepaid Expenses. The adjustment for prepaid expenses is typically the first kind of adjusting entry to be presented in an accounting course. These adjustments are usually included in the study of the first accounting cycle.

   1. Learning Outcomes. Students must be able to correctly analyze the available data to determine the adjusting entries required to update the prepaid expense accounts. Adjustment data could be given in the form of the amount of asset used/expired or the amount of asset remaining at the end of the period.

   2. Teaching Methods. Introduce adjustment analysis by illustrating what activities have been recorded in a prepaid expense account (such as supplies) during the current accounting period. The only activities that have been recorded are those showing the acquisition of supplies. A T account illustration of the Supplies account should be used.

SUPPLIES	
9-1 45	
13 25	
27 30	
Bal. 100	

Point out that even though supplies have been used by the business, no usage has been recorded in the account. Ask what would happen if the business kept recording the buying of supplies but ignoring the use of supplies. The desired answer is that the balance in the Supplies account will continue to increase, even though supplies are being bought and used.

Further explain the time and cost involved to make an entry every time supplies are used. The business can wait until the end of an accounting period to update (or adjust) the Supplies account because no financial statements are prepared until *after* the adjusting entries are made.

Once the reason for the adjustment is known, explain how the amount of the entry is determined. Someone in the business must determine the dollar amount of the supplies on hand at the end of the period, usually by taking a physical count of the asset. Assume the inventory of supplies indicates $30 worth of supplies are still on hand. Four questions can be asked to assist students.

1. What is the balance of the Supplies account? ($100)
2. What should the balance be for this account? ($ 30)
3. What must be done to correct the account balance? (Decrease the Supplies account $70)
4. What adjusting entry is necessary? (Debit Supplies Expense, $70 and credit Supplies, $70)

Explain that the amount of supplies used, $70, is an expense of the business for the current fiscal period; therefore, the Supplies Expense account is debited for $70. On the chalkboard or a transparency, illustrate a T account analysis of the adjusting entry and the balance of each account after the adjustment.

SUPPLIES				SUPPLIES EXPENSE	
9-1	45	9-30	70	9-30	70
13	25				
27	30				
Bal.	30			Bal.	70

Point out that the balance of the Supplies account is now $30, which is equal to the amount of supplies on hand. The balance of the Supplies Expense account, $70, represents the amount of supplies used in the current accounting period.

In order to emphasize the importance and purpose of adjusting entries, illustrate the effect the adjusting entry has on the financial statements. An example of the effects of the adjusting entry for supplies is given in Illustration 6–2.

Point out the difference between Total Assets if the adjustment is made and if the adjustment is not made. The related difference should be pointed out for Net Income. Re-emphasize the importance of identifying *all* of the accounts that need to be adjusted. If any accounts are *not* identified, both the balance sheet and the income statement will be incorrect.

Follow the same procedure to explain the adjustment for other prepaid expenses, such as Prepaid Insurance. As additional adjustments for prepaid expenses are discussed, require students to do more of the work individually. Ask more questions, gradually allowing students to determine the amount of the entry and the accounts affected. Similar drill problems should be assigned for individual completion.

BEFORE ADJUSTING ENTRY	AFTER ADJUSTING ENTRY
Partial Balance Sheet Lopez Secretarial Service September 30, 19—	Partial Balance Sheet Lopez Secretarial Service September 30, 19—
Assets	Assets
Cash $5,500.00 Supplies 100.00 Prepaid Ins. 600.00 Total Assets $6,200.00	Cash $5,500.00 Supplies 30.00 Prepaid Ins. 600.00 Total Assets $6,130.00
Income Statement Lopez Secretarial Service For Month Ended Sept 30, 19—	Income Statement Lopez Secretarial Service For Month Ended Sept 30, 19—

Revenue:
  Sales $2,200.00
Expenses:
  Adver. Exp. $300.00
  Util. Exp. 100.00
  Total Exp. 400.00
Net Income $1,800.00
	Revenue:
	  Sales $2,200.00
	Expenses:
	  Adver. Exp. $300.00
	  Supplies Exp. 70.00
	  Util. Exp. 100.00
	  Total Exp. 470.00
	Net Income $1,730.00

Illustration 6–2 Effects of the Adjusting Entry for Supplies

Second Cycle—Merchandise Inventory. The merchandise inventory adjustment is usually presented in the study of the second accounting cycle. The merchandise inventory adjustment is best done as a single adjusting entry for the difference between the balance in the account and the actual amount of merchandise on hand.

1. Learning Outcomes. Students must be able to correctly analyze the available data to determine the amount of the adjusting entry required to update the merchandise inventory account.

2. Teaching Methods. Follow the same general procedure as was discussed earlier regarding adjusting entries for prepaid expenses. Illustrate the T account for Merchandise Inventory on the chalkboard or a transparency.

MERCHANDISE INVENTORY	
1/1 35,000	

Explain that $35,000 represents the amount of merchandise that was on hand at the beginning of the accounting period. Ask if the amount of merchandise the business has on hand has changed during the year. The desired answer (Yes) should be followed with the question, "What caused the change?" The desired answer is that the business purchased merchandise from vendors and sold merchandise to customers. Point out that even though the amount of merchandise on hand has changed, the amount recorded in the Merchandise Inventory account has not changed.

Ask why the balance in the Merchandise Inventory account has not changed. The balance in the merchandise inventory account has not changed because when the business purchased merchandise, the account "Purchases" was debited. When the business sold merchandise, the account "Sales" was credited. Although both sales and purchase transactions affect the balance of Merchandise Inventory, neither transaction is recorded in the Merchandise Inventory account. In a periodic inventory system, the amount of inventory is not changed after each transaction affecting inventory.

Explain that when a periodic inventory system is used, the business must actually count the amount of merchandise on hand at the end of the accounting period. Counting inventory is the only way to determine how much merchandise is still on hand. Assume that a physical count has been taken and that there is $40,000 of inventory on hand.

Stress that once the inventory is counted, the Merchandise Inventory account must be updated or adjusted so that the balance equals the amount of inventory actually on hand. The amount of the adjustment is determined by answering the same four questions used above to determine the amount of the adjustment for prepaid expenses.

1. What is the balance of the Merchandise Inventory account? ($35,000)
2. What should the balance be for this account? ($40,000)
3. What must be done to correct the account balance? (Increase the Merchandise Inventory account $5,000)
4. What adjusting entry is necessary? (Debit Merchandise Inventory, $5,000 and credit Income Summary, $5,000)

Explain that the companion account for the merchandise inventory adjustment is the Income Summary account. Since students have already studied the closing process during the first presentation of the accounting cycle, the Income Summary account is not new. Remind students that the Income Summary account is used to summarize net income. Point out that the amount of inventory used during an accounting period does affect net income; therefore, the Income Summary account is used in the adjustment for Merchandise Inventory.

On the chalkboard or a transparency, illustrate a T account analysis of the adjusting entry and the balance of each account after the adjustment.

MERCHANDISE INVENTORY		INCOME SUMMARY	
1/1 35,000			12/31 5,000
12/31 5,000			
Bal. 40,000			

Point out that the balance of the Merchandise Inventory account is now $40,000, which is equal to the amount of inventory on hand. The balance of the Income Summary account, $5,000, will be included in the calculation of net income.

Illustrate the effect the adjusting entry has on the financial statements. (A format similar to the before/after example used for prepaid expenses is appropriate.) Showing the effect of the adjusting entry on the financial statements will emphasize the importance and the purpose of the adjusting entry and will serve as a review that every adjusting entry affects the balance sheet and the income statement.

Third Cycle—Contra Accounts: Bad Debts and Depreciation. The adjusting entries which affect contra accounts are usually covered in the study of the third accounting cycle. Bad debts and depreciation adjustments are somewhat more difficult for students to comprehend since the balance of an asset account is not actually decreased. Two commonly used contra accounts and their related asset accounts are: (a) Accumulated Depreciation and Equipment, and (b) Allowance for Uncollectible Accounts and Accounts Receivable.

1. Learning Outcomes. Students must be able to correctly analyze the available data to determine the amount of the adjusting entry required to fairly valuate the asset accounts.

2. Teaching Methods. Since accounting for contra accounts is generally presented in the last half of the first-year course, students will have had experience with adjusting entries before studying adjustments for bad debts and depreciation. However, contra account adjustments have some unique features and should be explained explicitly. In addition, build on previous learning when introducing contra account adjustments.

Before students can understand the entry for depreciation, the term depreciation and the reason for depreciation must be understood. Explain that depreciation is a method of spreading the cost of an asset (such as equipment) over the period of time the asset will be of service to the business. Since the equipment will help the business earn revenue over several accounting periods, the cost of the equipment must also be spread over the same number of accounting periods. Remind students of the accounting concept requiring the matching of revenues and expenses in the same fiscal period. The account used to record the amount of the cost each period is titled Depreciation Expense – Equipment.

Building on previous learning, introduce the contra adjustments by explaining that they are similar in many ways to the adjustment for prepaid expenses. Most importantly, an expense is increased and an asset is decreased in both types of adjusting entries.

After the similarities have been discussed, explain the major difference between the contra adjustment and the adjustment for prepaid expenses. Point out that assets remain on the financial records at the amount of the asset's original cost and cannot be credited in the adjusting entry (as was done in the supplies adjustment). Another account must be used to reduce a related account on a financial statement and is referred to as a contra account. The contra account used to record equipment depreciation is titled Accumulated Depreciation – Equipment. Whenever reported on financial statements, the book value of the asset (asset less contra account) is reported. T accounts can be used to illustrate related accounts. The balances in the related accounts on December 31, before adjusting entries have been recorded, are:

```
                    EQUIPMENT
    1/1         10,000
```

```
           ACCUMULATED DEPRECIATION—EQUIP
                        | 1/1          1,600
```

```
           DEPRECIATION EXPENSE—EQUIPMENT
```

The book value of the equipment before the adjustment is given in Illustration 6-3.

Once students understand the reason for the adjustment and the accounts affected, follow the same procedures to introduce the adjustment for prepaid expenses. Point out that students need to know the estimated equipment depreciation expense for the period. Once estimated depreciation is known, the four questions asked in previous adjustment analysis can be asked for the depreciation adjustment. Assume the yearly depreciation on the equipment is $400.00.

1. What is the balance of the Depreciation Expense – Equipment account? (zero)
2. What should the balance be for this account? ($400)
3. What must be done to correct the account balance? (Increase the Depreciation Expense – Equipment account $400)
4. What adjusting entry is necessary? (Debit Depreciation Expense – Equipment, $400 and credit Accumulated Depreciation – Equipment, $400)

The balances in the related accounts *after* the adjustment are:

```
                    EQUIPMENT
    1/1         10,000
```

```
           ACCUMULATED DEPRECIATION—EQUIP
                        | 1/1          1,600
                        | 12/31          400
                        | Bal.         2,000
```

```
           DEPRECIATION EXPENSE—EQUIPMENT
    12/21        400
```

Calculate the book value of the equipment before and after the adjustment to show the effect of the adjustment. The book value of the equipment is shown in Illustration 6–3.

	BEFORE ADJUSTMENT		AFTER ADJUSTMENT	
Equipment		$10,000.00	Equipment	$10,000.00
Less Accum. Depr.		1,600.00	Less Accum. Depr.	2,000.00
Equals Book Value 1-1		$ 8,400.00	Equals Book Value 12-31	$ 8,000.00

Illustration 6-3 Book Value Before and After Adjustment

Illustrate the effect the adjusting entry has on the financial statements. (A format similar to the before/after example used for prepaid expenses is appropriate.) Showing the effect of the adjusting entry on the financial statements will emphasize the importance and purpose of the adjusting entry and will serve as a review that every adjusting entry affects the balance sheet and the income statement.

Use a similar analysis to present the other major contra account adjustment, Allowance for Uncollectible Accounts and Bad Debts Expense.

Advanced Adjustments

More complex adjustments should be presented after students have a firm grasp of the previous adjustments. Advanced adjustments can be presented in the second semester of the first-year course but are more likely covered in the second-year course.

Prepaid Expenses Initially Recorded as an Expense. Some businesses initially record prepaid items, such as supplies and insurance, as expenses. If this approach is used, an adjusting entry is made at the end of the fiscal period to record the amount still prepaid or unused.

1. **Learning Outcomes.** Students must be able to correctly analyze previously recorded transactions and current account valuations to determine the amount of the adjusting entry and the accounts which need updating.

2. **Teaching Methods.** Students have already learned to analyze adjustments for prepaid expenses initially recorded as an asset. Previous knowledge should be used to illustrate the entry required to update the accounts. If $100 of supplies is initially recorded as an expense, the T accounts before adjustments would be:

SUPPLIES	SUPPLIES EXPENSE
	1/31 100

Assume that a count of the supplies determined that there is $30 of supplies on hand. Analyze the data using T accounts and the standard four questions.

1. What is the balance of the Supplies account? (zero)
2. What should the balance be for this account? ($30)
3. What must be done to correct the account balance? (Increase the Supplies account $30)
4. What adjusting entry is necessary? (Debit Supplies, $30 and credit Supplies Expense, $30)

After the analysis is completed, compare the two methods of accounting for prepaid expenses on the chalkboard or transparency. Prepare a transparency similar to Illustration 6–4 to show the comparison. Stress that *after* the adjustment is made, the account balances for Supplies and Supplies Expense are the same for both methods.

	RECORDED INITIALLY AS AN ASSET	RECORDED INITIALLY AS AN EXPENSE
BEFORE ADJUSTMENT	SUPPLIES 1/31 100	SUPPLIES
	SUPPLIES EXPENSE	SUPPLIES EXPENSE 1/31 100
AFTER ADJUSTMENT	SUPPLIES 1/31 100 | 1/31 70 Bal. 30	SUPPLIES 1/31 30
	SUPPLIES EXPENSE 1/31 70	SUPPLIES EXPENSE 1/31 100 | 1/31 30 Bal. 70

Illustration 6–4
Comparison of Two Methods to Record and Adjust Prepaid Expense Accounts

Illustrate the effect the adjusting entry has on the financial statements. (A format similar to the before/after example used for prepaid expenses initially recorded as an asset is appropriate.) Showing the effect of the adjusting entry on the financial statements will emphasize the importance and purpose of the adjusting entry and will serve as a review that every adjusting entry affects the balance sheet and the income statement.

Unearned Revenue Initially Recorded as a Liability. Some businesses initially record unearned revenues as a liability and adjust the account to reflect revenue earned at the end of the fiscal period.

1. Learning Outcomes. Students must be able to compare the balance of the unearned revenue (liability) account with the amount of revenue earned to correctly determine the amount of the required adjusting entry. In addition, students must be able to identify the accounts affected by the adjustment.

2. Teaching Methods. Review the adjustment for a prepaid expense initially recorded as a liability. Explain that with a prepaid expense, the adjustment brings an asset account, such as Supplies, up to date and records the adjustment in an expense account, such as Supplies Expense. Point out that an adjustment for unearned revenue is similar but uses liability and revenue accounts.

Use T accounts to help students understand the previously recorded transaction.

CASH		UNEARNED RENT	
3/1 3,600			3/1 3,600

Explain that when the business received the cash it had not yet earned the revenue so the transaction was recorded as a liability. Once the business has earned some of the revenue, the adjustment must bring the liability account, Unearned Rent, up to date to reflect the amount of revenue still *unearned*. The adjustment must also record the amount of revenue now earned in the revenue account, Rent Income. Assume that $3,000 of revenue has been earned.

Analyze the data using T accounts and the standard four questions.

1. What is the balance of the Unearned Rent account? ($3,600)
2. What should the balance be for this account? ($600)
3. What must be done to correct the account balance? (Decrease the Unearned Rent account $3,000)
4. What adjusting entry is necessary? (Debit Unearned Rent, $3,000 and credit Rent Income, $3,000)

The balances in the related accounts *after* the adjustment are:

UNEARNED RENT				RENT INCOME	
12/31 3,000	3/1 3,600				12/31 3,000
	Bal. 600				

Place the T account analysis on the chalkboard or on a transparency. Illustrate the effect the adjusting entry has on the financial statements. (A format similar to the before/after example used for prepaid expenses is appropriate.) Showing the effect of the adjusting entry on the financial statements will emphasize the importance and purpose of the adjusting entry and will serve as a review that every adjusting entry affects the balance sheet and the income statement.

Unearned Revenue Initially Recorded as a Revenue. Some businesses initially record unearned revenue as a revenue. If this approach is used, an adjusting entry is made at the end of the fiscal period to record the amount still unearned.

1. Learning Outcomes. Students must be able to correctly analyze previously recorded transactions and current account valuations to determine the amount of the adjusting entry and the accounts which need updating.

2. Teaching Methods. Students have already learned to analyze adjustments for unearned revenue initially recorded as a liability. Previous knowledge should be used to illustrate the entry required to update the accounts. If $3,600 of unearned revenue is initially recorded as a revenue, the T accounts before the adjustment would be:

UNEARNED RENT		RENT INCOME	
		3/1	3,600

Assume that $3,000 of revenue has been earned. Analyze the data using T accounts and the standard four questions.

1. What is the balance of the Unearned Rent account? (zero)
2. What should the balance be for this account? ($600)
3. What must be done to correct the account balance? (Increase the Unearned Rent account $600)
4. What adjusting entry is necessary? (Debit Rent Income, $600 and credit Unearned Rent, $600)

After the analysis is completed, compare the two methods of accounting for unearned revenues on the chalkboard or transparency. Prepare a transparency similar to Illustration 6–5 to show the comparison. Stress that *after* the adjustment is made, the account balances for Unearned Rent and Rent Income are the same for both methods.

	RECORDED INITIALLY AS A LIABILITY	RECORDED INITIALLY AS A REVENUE
BEFORE ADJUSTMENT	UNEARNED RENT 3/1 3,600	UNEARNED RENT
	RENT INCOME	RENT INCOME 3/1 3,600
AFTER ADJUSTMENT	UNEARNED RENT 12/31 3,000 | 3/1 3,600 Bal. 600	UNEARNED RENT 12/31 600
	RENT INCOME 12/31 3,000	RENT INCOME 12/31 600 | 3/1 3,600 Bal. 3,000

Illustration 6–5
Comparison of Two Methods to Record and Adjust Unearned Revenue Accounts

Illustrate the effect the adjusting entry has on the financial statements. (A format similar to the before/after example used for prepaid expenses is appropriate.) Showing the effect of the adjusting entry on the financial statements will emphasize the importance and purpose of the adjusting entry and will serve as a review that every adjusting entry affects the balance sheet and the income statement.

Accrued Expenses. An accrued expense is one that is incurred in one fiscal period but not paid until the next fiscal period. Some common expenses that frequently are accrued at the end of a fiscal period are interest expense, salary expense, and payroll expenses.

1. Learning Outcomes. Students must be able to calculate the amount of accrued expense and identify the accounts affected to correctly determine the required adjusting entry.

2. Teaching Methods. As the first step in teaching the analysis of adjustments for accrued expenses, lead a directed class discussion. The discussion should be used to clarify what accrued expenses are and how they are generally used. Several points need to be emphasized: (1) Accrued expenses are expenses that have been incurred but have not yet been paid. (2) An adjustment must be made to bring the accounts up to date. (3) The adjustment will recognize the expense incurred and the liability the business now has for the accrued expense.

Before the adjusting entry can be analyzed, the amount of the expense must be calculated. Make a transparency of Illustration 6-6, and use the example to demonstrate how the amount of interest expense should be calculated.

CALCULATING ACCRUED EXPENSE

On July 1, Ludden Co. issued a one-year note payable: principal, $5,000; 12% interest. On December 31, the company owes accrued interest for six months.

Interest calculation: Principle × Rate of interest × Length of time
                           5,000   ×   .12   ×   6/12

Interest = $300.00

Illustration 6-6 Calculating Accrued Expense

The procedure used to analyze all previous adjustments should be used to analyze the accrued expense adjustment. Since no entry has been recorded, the balances in the T accounts are zero:

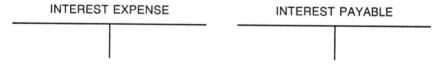

Analyze the data using T accounts and the standard four questions.

1. What is the balance of the Interest Payable account? (zero)
2. What should the balance be for this account? ($300)
3. What must be done to correct the account balance? (Increase the Interest Payable account $300)
4. What adjusting entry is necessary? (Debit Interest Expense, $300 and credit Interest Payable, $300)

The balances in the related accounts *after* the adjustment are:

INTEREST EXPENSE	INTEREST PAYABLE
12/31 300	12/31 300

Illustrate the effect the adjusting entry has on the financial statements. (A format similar to the before/after example used for prepaid expenses is appropriate.) Showing the effect of the adjusting entry on the financial statements will emphasize the importance and purpose of the adjusting entry and will serve as a review that every adjusting entry affects the balance sheet and the income statement.

Accrued Revenues. An accrued revenue is one that is earned in one fiscal period but not received until the next fiscal period. A common revenue account that frequently is accrued at the end of a fiscal period is interest revenue.

1. **Learning Outcomes.** Students must be able to calculate the amount of accrued revenue and identify the accounts affected to correctly determine the required adjusting entry.

2. **Teaching Methods.** Explain that the adjustment for accrued revenue is similar to the adjustment for accrued expense. The principal difference is that accrued expenses involve expense and liability accounts whereas accrued revenues involve revenue and asset accounts. Consequently, the accrued revenue adjustment should be analyzed in the same way that the accrued expense adjustment is analyzed.

Proceed step-by-step through the analysis as previously listed for the accrued expense analysis.

Planning Adjustments on a Work Sheet

A work sheet is used to plan adjustments. Changes are not made in general ledger accounts until adjustments are journalized and posted. The accuracy of planning for adjustments is checked on a work sheet before adjustments are actually journalized.

Learning Outcomes. Students must be able to correctly enter the planned adjustment on a work sheet. After the adjustments are recorded on the work sheet, students must be able to prove the equality of the adjustments by totaling the adjustment columns.

Teaching Methods. As soon as each adjusting entry is analyzed, the amount of the entry should be written on the work sheet in the adjustment column. Demonstrate the procedure for planning adjustments on a work sheet after *each* adjusting entry is analyzed. Display a work sheet transparency similar to Illustration 6–7 with the heading and trial balance previously recorded. Each student should be given a copy of the transparency to complete along with the instructor.

After each account needing adjustment has been analyzed, record on the transparency (1) the debit amount, (2) the credit amount, and (3) the letter of the debit and credit entry labeling the adjusting entry. Emphasize the importance of following the same procedure for each adjustment as a precaution against omitting a step.

After all adjustments have been analyzed and recorded on the work sheet, total the debit and credit adjustment columns. If the totals are equal, they should be recorded on the work sheet. Finally, rule the debit and credit adjustment columns with a double line. Stress the importance of the debit column total equaling the credit column total before continuing with the work sheet.

Lopez Secretarial Service
Work Sheet
For Month Ended June 30, 19—

Account Title	Trial Balance		Adjustments	
	Debit	Credit	Debit	Credit
Cash	5,500.00			
Supplies	100.00			(a) 70.00
Prepaid Insurance	600.00			
Buscher Paper Supply		500.00		
Morse Janitorial Supplies		800.00		
Martin Lopez, Capital		2,400.00		
Martin Lopez, Drawing		700.00		
Sales		2,200.00		
Advertising Expense	300.00			
Insurance Expense				
Supplies Expense			(a) 70.00	
Utilities Expense	100.00			
	6,600.00	6,600.00	70.00	70.00

Illustration 6-7 Trial Balance and Adjustment Columns of a Work Sheet

Completing a Work Sheet

The work sheet is also used to separate general ledger account balances according to the financial statements to be prepared and to figure the amount of net income or net loss for the fiscal period.

Learning Outcomes. After all necessary adjustments are entered on a work sheet, students must be able to complete the work sheet. Completing the work sheet includes extending the balance of each account to the appropriate income statement or balance sheet column, figuring and recording net income or net loss, and totaling and ruling the work sheet.

Teaching Methods. Demonstrate completing the work sheet by following three major steps. (1) Extend account balances to either the income statement or balance sheet columns. Explain how new account balances should be calculated for those accounts adjusted in the adjustment columns. (2) Figure and record net income or net loss in the income statement and balance sheet columns. (3) Total and rule the income statement and balance sheet columns. Use a transparency of a work sheet with adjustments already entered to show how the work sheet is completed. Give each student a copy of the transparency to complete along with the instructor. Ask students at random to tell how each account balance is extended. As correct responses are given, record the extension on the transparency.

To reinforce understanding of correct account balance extension procedures on a work sheet, display a transparency similar to Illustration 6–8 with account titles listed. Point to one account at a time and randomly ask individual students to determine and state (1) in which Trial Balance column the account balance is recorded and (2) to which column the balance is extended. Place check marks in the appropriate columns as correct responses are given.

	1	2	3	4	5	6
	Trial Balance		Income Statement		Balance Sheet	
Account Title	Debit	Credit	Debit	Credit	Debit	Credit
1. Advertising Expense	✓		✓			
2. Office Equipment	✓				✓	
3. Rent Expense	✓		✓			
4. Brown Supply Company (liability)		✓				✓
5. Utilities Expense	✓		✓			
6. Cash	✓				✓	
7. Roger Arnold, Capital		✓				✓
8. Sales		✓		✓		
9. Miscellaneous Expense	✓		✓			
10. Supplies	✓				✓	
11. Roger Arnold, Drawing	✓				✓	

Illustration 6–8   Account Balance Extension Drill

When all account balances have been extended on the transparency of the work sheet, rule a single line across the Income Statement and Balance Sheet columns. Ask students to total each of the columns. From two or three student responses, determine and record the totals for each column.

Next, ask what kind of accounts are listed in the Income Statement Debit column (expense) and Income Statement Credit column (revenue). State that the total of the Income Statement Debit column is the total of all expenses for the accounting period. Similarly, the total of the Income Statement Credit column is the total of all revenue for the accounting period. Ask what is calculated by the formula "Revenue - Expenses" (net income). Stress that the difference between the Income Statement Debit and Credit columns must equal the net income or net loss for the accounting period.

Demonstrate writing the amount of the net income or net loss below the column totals on the side with the smaller total. Draw a single rule across both money columns below the net income figure and determine new column totals. Since these two column totals are now equal, double rule the Income Statement Debit and Credit columns.

To complete the Balance Sheet columns (assuming a net income), ask what effect net income has on owner's equity. The desired answer is that net income increases owner's equity. Stress that since net income increases owner's equity and since owner's equity increases on the credit side, the amount of the net income is written in the Balance Sheet Credit column below the total. Draw a single rule across both Balance Sheet columns below the net income figure and determine new column totals. Since these two column totals are now equal, double rule the Balance Sheet Debit and Credit columns.

Follow the same procedures to demonstrate how to complete the Balance Sheet columns for a work sheet containing a net loss.

To reinforce student understanding of the procedure for calculating net income or net loss and completing the work sheet, display a transparency similar to Illustration 6–9 with Income Statement and Balance Sheet column totals before net income (or loss) is figured. Have each student figure the net income for each company. Individual students should be called on to give the amount of net income or loss and to explain how to complete the work sheet. Record correct answers on the transparency.

	Income Statement		Balance Sheet	
	Debit	Credit	Debit	Credit
COMPANY 1				
1.	$4,500.00	$5,300.00	$36,670.00	$35,870.00
2. Net Income	800.00			800.00
3.	$5,300.00	$5,300.00	$36,670.00	$36,670.00
COMPANY 2				
1.	$974.00	$2,186.00	$7,937.00	$6,725.00
2. Net Income	1212.00			1212.00
3.	$2,186.00	$2,186.00	$7,937.00	$7,937.00
COMPANY 3				
1.	$4,050.00	$3,994.00	$25,669.00	$25,725.00
2. Net Loss		56.00	56.00	
3.	$4,050.00	$4,050.00	$25,725.00	$25,725.00
COMPANY 4				
1.	$4,192.00	$5,265.00	$33,442.00	$32,369.00
2. Net Income	1073.00			1073.00
3.	$5,265.00	$5,265.00	$33,442.00	$33,442.00

Illustration 6–9   Drill on Calculating Net Income (Loss) on a Work Sheet and Completing the Work Sheet

Note: If a 10-column work sheet is used instead of the usual 8-column work sheet, explain how every trial balance amount is extended to the Adjusted Trial Balance Debit or Credit column. The same procedures used above can be used to demonstrate how the amounts in the Adjusted Trial Balance columns are used to extend amounts to the Income Statement or Balance Sheet columns. Use the procedures above to explain how to complete the work sheet.

GENERAL CONSIDERATIONS

Adjusting entries are encountered throughout the accounting course. Simple adjusting entries for prepaid expenses are usually introduced first. As each new adjustment is presented, build on previous knowledge so that students will see the similarity between adjusting entries.

Use the same procedure for analyzing each adjustment. By following a logical procedure during presentations, students are provided with a tool that can be used to analyze any adjustment. Generally, the procedure for analyzing adjustments is to (1) explain the purpose of and the need for the adjustment, (2) use T accounts to illustrate the balance in the accounts before the adjustment, (3) use the four questions to determine the adjusting entry, (4) use T accounts to illustrate the balance in the accounts after the adjustment, and (5) illustrate the financial statements before and after the adjusting entry to emphasize how the entries affect the financial statements. In addition, when a second method for an adjustment is being presented, compare the two methods side by side so that students can see that the result is the same in either case.

The use of flash cards is especially appropriate for the topic of adjusting entries. In order to provide practice for students to quickly identify accounts normally adjusted, prepare each flash card with an account title. Use the cards to check student response in a number of ways. (1) An account title is flashed and students respond with either "Adjust" or "Don't adjust." (2) An account title is flashed and students respond with the name of the companion account or "Don't adjust." (3) A student is called on individually to respond with either of the two choices above.

Flash cards can also be used to drill students on extending amounts to the appropriate work sheet columns. Account titles should be written on the front of cards. As the cards are flashed, students must identify (1) either income statement or balance sheet and (2) debit or credit.

Finally, the use of bulletin boards is helpful while presenting adjusting entries and work sheets. Bulletin boards can be prepared to illustrate (1) the T accounts before and after any kind of adjusting entry is recorded, (2) the comparison of two different methods of adjusting certain accounts, (3) how to record adjusting entries on the work sheet, and (4) how to complete the work sheet.

CHAPTER 7
TEACHING FINANCIAL STATEMENTS AND ANALYSIS

The definition of an accounting system can be stated as "a planned process for providing financial information that will be useful to management." The financial information provided is generally presented in the form of financial statements. Financial statements are like a newspaper or newsletter, communicating essential financial elements of a business in a clear and concise fashion. The financial statements of a business justify the existence of the accounting system.

As important as financial statements are, the statements are of no value if they are not used. Financial statements provide owners and managers with the information necessary to make financial decisions and are also used to prepare reports for federal and state governments, lending agencies, and owners.

ESSENTIAL ELEMENTS OF FINANCIAL STATEMENTS AND ANALYSIS

The preparation and analysis of financial statements are discussed in numerous chapters throughout an accounting course, rather than being isolated in a single chapter. The following activities comprise the elements which are essential to the understanding of the preparation and analysis of financial statements.

Preparing an Income Statement

An income statement reports the financial progress of a business by showing if the business is earning a profit or a loss.

Learning Outcomes. Students must be able to prepare income statements in a commonly accepted form. Throughout the accounting course, students must prepare income statements for a variety of businesses, including (1) a service business owned as a single proprietorship, (2) a merchandising business owned as a partnership, and (3) a merchandising business owned as a corporation.

Teaching Methods. An income statement prepared for a service business is the simplest form of income statement and should be presented first in the accounting course. Introduce the income statement by explaining that it is used to determine how profitable the business was for the fiscal period. Profitability is stated in terms of the amount of net income or net loss for the period.

It should be stressed that work sheets are used to prepare all financial statements.

Distribute copies of a sheet containing (1) a partial work sheet completed previously in class, similar to the top half of Illustration 7-1, and (2) a blank income statement form. Illustrate the income statement on the chalkboard or transparency while students individually complete the income statement on the blank form.

Turner's Tanning Salon
Work Sheet
For Month Ended July 31, 19—

Account Title	Income Statement Debit	Income Statement Credit	Balance Sheet Debit	Balance Sheet Credit
Cash			3,137.00	
Supplies			850.00	
Prepaid Insurance			590.00	
Newell Supply Company				250.00
Quality Equipment Company				200.00
Judy Turner, Capital				1,650.00
Judy Turner, Drawing			1,000.00	
Sales		5,199.00		
Advertising Expense	200.00			
Maintenance Expense	170.00			
Rent Expense	1,000.00			
Utilities Expense	352.00			
	1,722.00	5,199.00	5,577.00	2,100.00
Net Income	3,477.00			3,477.00
	5,199.00	5,199.00	5,577.00	5,577.00

Turner Tanning Salon
Income Statement
For Month Ended July 31, 19—

Revenue:		
Sales		5,199.00
Expenses:		
Advertising Expense	200.00	
Maintenance Expense	170.00	
Rent Expense	1,000.00	
Utilities Expense	352.00	
Total Expenses		1,722.00
Net Income		3,477.00

Illustration 7-1 Work Sheet Columns Needed to Prepare Financial Statements and a Completed Income Statement for a Service Business

The income statement is prepared by using the Income Statement columns of the work sheet. If the income statement is the first financial statement students have prepared, point out that all financial statements begin with a heading that answers three questions: who, what, and when. Stress that the "when" on an income statement is a period of time.

Explain that there are three sections on an income statement. The first section is titled "Revenue." The balance of each revenue account is listed in the revenue section. Ask students to look at the work sheet and identify the revenue account(s). When the correct answer is given, enter the account title "Sales" and the amount of sales, $5,199.00. Since there is only one revenue account, there is no need to total the revenue section of the income statement.

The second section of the income statement is titled "Expenses." The balance of each expense account is listed in the expense section. Ask students to look at the work sheet and identify the expense accounts. As each account is given, enter the account title and the amount of the balance. After all expense account balances have been copied, illustrate how to total the expense section.

The third section of the income statement is titled "Net Income" or "Net Loss." Explain that the formula to calculate net income(loss) is:

REVENUE − EXPENSES = NET INCOME(LOSS)

Ask students to determine the amount of net income or loss. Solicit answers from several students to obtain the correct amount of net income. Enter the heading "Net Income" and the amount of the net income on the income statement. Finally, double rule across both money columns.

When introducing the income statement for a merchandising business, first review the income statement format for a service business. Build on previous knowledge by pointing out how the income statement for a merchandising business is different.

Give special attention to the new cost of merchandise sold section. Write the calculations for the cost of merchandise sold section on the chalkboard.

```
    Beginning Merchandise Inventory
  + Purchases
    _____
  = Merchandise Available for Sale
  − Ending Merchandise Inventory
    _____
  = Cost of Merchandise Sold
```

Since the cost of merchandise sold section is a new section of the income statement, drill students on how the cost of merchandise sold is figured. Use an exercise similar to that given in Illustration 7–2, on page 82.

The remaining sections of the income statement for a merchandising business are similar to those for a service business. Follow the same procedure used to explain the preparation of an income statement for a service business.

If other forms of income statements are presented in the accounting course, such as one with a classified expense section, always present a familiar income statement first and then introduce the new section, pointing out the similarities and differences in a step by step manner.

Bus.	Account Title	Trial Balance		Income Statement		Balance Sheet	
		Debit	Credit	Debit	Credit	Debit	Credit
1	Mdse. Inventory	35,000				40,000	
	Purchases			17,000			
2	Mdse. Inventory	15,500				12,000	
	Purchases			20,000			
3	Mdse. Inventory	9,000				11,800	
	Purchases			35,000			

Directions: Calculate the cost of merchandise sold for each business.

Answers: Business 1 _____

   Business 2 _____

   Business 3 _____

Illustration 7-2   Drill on Calculating Cost of Merchandise Sold

Preparing an Owners' or Stockholder's Equity Statement

An owners' equity statement summarizes the changes in equity during the current fiscal period and shows if the owners' equity is increasing or decreasing and the reasons for the change.

Learning Outcomes. Students must be able to prepare equity statements in a commonly accepted form. Throughout the accounting course, students must prepare equity statements for a variety of businesses, including single proprietorships, partnerships, and corporations. Students must also be able to prepare equity statements which include additional investments and/or withdrawals as well as a net income or net loss for the fiscal period.

Teaching Methods. An equity statement prepared for a single proprietorship is the simplest form of equity statement and should be presented first in the accounting course. Introduce the equity statement by explaining that it is used to summarize the changes in owner's equity during a fiscal period. Business owners can review an equity statement to determine if the owner's equity is increasing or decreasing and what is causing the change.

Relying on previous knowledge, ask students where the information for financial statements is obtained. Students should remember that the work sheet is the source of information for financial statements. Add that additional information from the owner's capital account may also be necessary.

Distribute copies of a sheet containing (1) a partial work sheet completed previously in class, similar to the top half of Illustration 7-1, and (2) a blank owner's equity statement form. Illustrate the owner's equity statement on the chalkboard or transparency while students individually complete the owner's equity statement on the blank form.

Next, ask students what three questions are answered by the heading on a financial statement. Using previous knowledge, students should be able to give the desired answer: who, what, and when. Write the heading on the form, pointing out that the owner's equity statement covers the same period of time as the accounting period.

From information on the transparency, complete the owner's equity statement, explaining the source of each line. The completed owner's equity statement is given in Illustration 7-3.

Turner Tanning Salon
Owner's Equity Statement
For Month Ended July 31, 19—

Judy Turner, Capital July 1, 19—		1,650.00
Net Income for July	3,477.00	
Less: Judy Turner, Drawing	1,000.00	
Net Increase in Capital		2,477.00
Judy Turner, Capital July 31, 19—		4,127.00

Illustration 7-3 Owner's Equity Statement for a Single Proprietorship

Also explain how the owner's equity statement would be different if there were additional investments and/or a net loss for the period. Emphasize, however, that the basic statement does not change. This procedure will help prepare students for more complex equity statements later in the accounting course.

When equity statements for partnerships and corporations are presented, use the simple form of equity statement to review previous knowledge. Stress the similarities between the previous and the new equity statements. Next, point out the differences between the two equity statements so that students will see the connection between equity statements and will more easily understand and remember the various forms of equity statements.

Preparing a Balance Sheet

A balance sheet reports the financial condition of a business. A balance sheet shows if the business is financially strong.

Learning Outcomes. Students must be able to prepare balance sheets in a commonly accepted form. Throughout the accounting course, students must prepare balance sheets for a variety of businesses, including single proprietorships, partnerships, and corporations. In addition, students should be able to use both the account format and the report format to prepare balance sheets.

Teaching Methods. A balance sheet prepared for a single proprietorship is the simplest form of balance sheet and should be presented first in the accounting course. Introduce the balance sheet by explaining that it is used to report the financial condition of a business by showing if the business is financially strong.

Relying on previous knowledge, ask students where the information for financial statements is obtained. Students should remember that the work sheet is the source of information for financial statements. Point out that information from the owner's equity statement is also necessary to complete a balance sheet.

Distribute copies of a sheet containing (1) a partial work sheet completed previously in class, similar to the top half of Illustration 7–1, (2) the completed owner's equity statement prepared above, Illustration 7–3, and (3) a blank balance sheet form. Illustrate the balance sheet on the chalkboard or transparency while students individually complete the balance sheet on the blank form.

Next, ask students what three questions are answered by the heading on a financial statement. Using previous knowledge, students should be able to give the desired answer: who, what, and when. Write the heading on the form, pointing out that the balance sheet is for a specific date, the last day of the accounting period.

Stress the relationship between the accounting equation and the account form of a balance sheet. Write the accounting equation on the chalkboard and put the skeleton of a balance sheet below it:

ASSETS	=	LIABILITIES + OWNER'S EQUITY
Assets		Liabilities
		Owner's Equity

From information on the transparency, complete the balance sheet, explaining the source of each line. Stress that the amount entered for Judy Turner, Capital is the ending balance as found on the owner's equity statement. The completed balance sheet is given in Illustration 7–4.

Turner Tanning Salon
Balance Sheet
July 31, 19—

Assets		Liabilities	
Cash	3,137.00	Newell Supply Company	250.00
Supplies	850.00	Quality Equipment Company	200.00
Prepaid Insurance	590.00	Total Liabilities	450.00
		Capital	
		Judy Turner, Capital	4,127.00
Total Assets	4,577.00	Total Liab. and O.E.	4,577.00

Illustration 7–4 Completed Balance Sheet for a Single Proprietorship

Explain that the balance sheet is in account form. At some point in the accounting course students should learn how to prepare a balance sheet in report form. When the report form of balance sheet is presented, emphasize the similarities between the account form and the report form. Next, point out the differences between the two forms. Finally, display the two formats side-by-side, allowing students to visually compare the formats.

When classified balance sheets or balance sheets for partnerships and corporations are presented, use the simple form of balance sheet to review previous knowledge.

Stress the similarities between the previous and the new balance sheets. Next, point out the differences so that students will see the connection between balance sheets and will more easily understand and remember the various forms of balance sheets.

Analyzing Financial Statements

The process of using financial statements to make business decisions is generally called "analyzing the financial statements." The amounts on the financial statements must be studied and compared to other amounts on current and prior financial statements. Standard calculations have been developed that show the relationship between amounts on the financial statements, allowing users to make knowledgeable decisions about the operations of the business.

Learning Outcomes. Students must be able to perform and interpret common financial statement calculations. Income statement calculations include component percentages for all amounts. Balance sheet calculations include working capital and the current ratio. In addition, students must be able to use the results of financial statement calculations to make decisions for the business.

Teaching Methods. Immediately after the presentation on how to prepare each financial statement, introduce the topic of financial statement analysis so that students will realize that preparing financial statements is *not* the last step in the accounting cycle. In order to make sound financial decisions, the prepared financial statements must be analyzed.

The first presentation of financial statement analysis should be simple and easy to apply. A common financial statement calculation is the ratio of net income to net sales. This is a good ratio to use to introduce the topic of financial analysis. On a transparency or the chalkboard, display an income statement similar to that given in Illustration 7–5.

Simpson Sign Company
Income Statement
For Year Ended December 31, 19X2

Revenue:		
Sales		20,000.00
Expenses:		
Insurance Expense	1,000.00	
Salaries Expense	8,600.00	
Utilities Expense	5,400.00	
Total Expenses		15,000.00
Net Income		5,000.00

Illustration 7–5   Income Statement

Explain that the ratio of net income to net sales calculates the relationship between net income and net sales. Use the income statement in Illustration 7–5 to demonstrate this calculation:

$$\frac{\text{Net Income}}{\text{Net Sales}} \quad \text{or} \quad \frac{5000}{20000} \quad \text{or} \quad .25$$

Further explain that the relationship between net income and net sales can be expressed in three ways: (1) as a ratio, such as .25 times or .25 to 1, (2) as a percentage, such as 25%, and (3) as a fraction, such as 1/4. The ratio of income to sales is commonly expressed as a percentage. In the previous example, it can be said that the ratio of income to sales is 25% or that net income is 25% of sales. The ratio also means that for each dollar of sales, Simpson earns 25 cents of net income.

Stress that most often the ratio itself is not meaningful. In order to be meaningful, the business would compare the ratio to similar ratios. The current year's ratio could be compared to that of previous years or to the average ratios for other businesses in the same industry.

To illustrate comparing prior period ratios, display Simpson Sign Company's income statement from the previous year, as given in Illustration 7–6.

Simpson Sign Company
Income Statement
For Year Ended December 31, 19X1

Revenue:		
Sales		15,000.00
Expenses:		
Insurance Expense	700.00	
Salaries Expense	6,900.00	
Utilities Expense	3,200.00	
Total Expenses		10,800.00
Net Income		4,200.00

Illustration 7–6 Income Statement from Previous Year

Students should be able to calculate the net income to net sales ratio individually. Ask two or three students to state the ratio. After determining that the ratio is 28%, point out that the ratio decreased from the previous year by 3%. Last year, Simpson made 28 cents of net income for every dollar of sales. Stress that the trend is not good. A business should attempt to improve its ratio from one period to the next.

Also point out that even though the amount of net income increased in the current year, the net income to net sales ratio trend is negative. Comparing income statements by looking only at dollar amounts can be misleading; therefore, ratios are calculated to assist in the comparison.

The business could also acquire the average ratio for other businesses in the same industry, which is referred to as the industry average. Industrial organizations publish industry averages for various types of businesses. By obtaining the industry average, Simpson Sign Company can determine how its ratio compares to other businesses in the sign industry.

Another common ratio is the ratio of gross profit to net sales. Use the previously stated procedure to present the gross profit ratio. Throughout the accounting course, each amount on the income statement should be divided by net sales to determine a ratio for each component of the income statement. Each component percentage should be introduced by following the above procedure.

When classified balance sheets are introduced in the accounting course, explain that financial statement calculations are also performed on balance sheet amounts. One of the easiest calculations is the working capital of the business. In order to understand the working capital calculation, students must know the definition of current assets and current liabilities. Cash and assets readily exchanged for cash or consumed within a year are known as current assets. Liabilities due within a short time, usually within a year, are known as current liabilities. The formula used to determine working capital is:

$$\text{Current Assets} - \text{Current Liabilities} = \text{Working Capital}$$

Explain that working capital is the amount of financial resources the business has available to conduct its daily operations. For a company to operate efficiently, it must have an adequate supply of resources remaining after current liabilities are paid.

If Simpson Sign Company has current assets of $7,888.00 and current liabilities of 3,543.00, Simpson's working capital can be calculated as:

$$7,888.00 - 3,543.00 = 4,345.00$$

Point out that working capital should not be confused with cash. Simpson does *not* have $4,345.00 extra cash after current liabilities are paid. However, Simpson does have $7,888.00 of assets which could be converted to cash and could be available to use in daily operations during the next year.

As with component ratios, the amount of working capital alone is not as meaningful as when the current working capital can be compared with prior years' working capital or with the industry average. Again, stress that a business is concerned with the trend its working capital is following. Is working capital decreasing or increasing? How does the increase/decrease compare with the industry average? Point out that an increase in working capital is usually a favorable condition.

Another calculation performed on the balance sheet amounts is the current ratio. The current ratio compares the amount of total current assets to total current liabilities. The calculation for current ratio is:

$$\frac{\text{Current Assets}}{\text{Current Liabilities}}$$

Point out that the current ratio is a useful measure of the business's ability to pay its current liabilities. Using the amounts given above, Simpson's current ratio would be:

$$\frac{7,888.00}{3,543.00} \text{ or } 2.226 \text{ or } 2.23 \text{ times}$$

Using Simpson's current ratio as an example, it could be said that Simpson's current liabilities could be paid 2.23 times by Simpson's current assets. As with other calculations, the current ratio must be compared with the current ratio from prior years or with industry averages to determine if Simpson's trend is positive or negative.

For each financial statement calculation, explain the meaning and the use of the calculation. Students should be given the opportunity to determine *and* interpret common financial statement calculations, so financial statement analysis should be introduced early. At the end of the first accounting cycle, for instance, introduce one or two income statement ratios. Stress that the financial statements alone are of little value. Only by *analyzing* the financial statements can the business make good financial decisions.

Financial statement analysis is an excellent opportunity to combine accounting skill and knowledge with written communications. Distribute a set of financial statements for a business. Ask students to calculate component percentages, working capital, and current ratio. In addition, students should discuss, in writing, what the results mean and explain any trends that may be occurring.

Also, use financial statement analysis to introduce case studies to the accounting curriculum. Cases can involve financial statement analysis and can either be given in the form of a written assignment or used in a class discussion.

To make financial statement analysis more realistic, gather financial statements from local and national businesses.

Financial statement analysis is also a good time to introduce students to the idea of estimating in order to determine if the answer is logical or not. Students should be taught to look at the numbers in a formula and roughly estimate the answer to see if it is reasonable or not. Stress that estimating can uncover a mathematical error made in a calculation.

Finally, the topic of financial statement analysis presents an opportunity to invite various guest speakers into the accounting classroom to discuss how financial statement analysis is used in their jobs. Bankers, managers, school officials, and city administrators are good candidates for this discussion.

GENERAL CONSIDERATIONS

When teaching students how to prepare financial statements, take care to model good methods. Financial statements should be neat and accurate. A single rule should be drawn through any error, with the correction written above the error. All rulings should be straight.

Help students see the overall format of each financial statement so that students will realize there is some flexibility within the confines of commonly acceptable formats.

Bulletin boards can be used extensively throughout these topics. Each financial statement (and the work sheet as its source) can be illustrated on a bulletin board. To reinforce how to analyze financial statements, calculations can also be displayed on a bulletin board.

After each financial statement is introduced, students should be given the opportunity to practice preparing that financial statement on an individual basis.

Finally, throughout financial statement preparation and analysis, focus on the *why* of accounting: Why prepare an income statement, an owner's equity statement, or a balance sheet? Why analyze the financial statements? By concentrating on *why*, students will understand and appreciate the importance of financial statements for a business.

CHAPTER 8
TEACHING RECORDING OF ADJUSTING, CLOSING AND REVERSING ENTRIES

Adjusting, closing, and reversing entries make up the last of the end-of-fiscal-period work that must be completed each fiscal period. End-of-fiscal-period work updates the account balances, closes the temporary accounts, transfers net income/loss and owner's drawing into the capital account, and prepares the accounts for the next fiscal period.

ESSENTIAL ELEMENTS OF ADJUSTING, CLOSING, AND REVERSING ENTRIES

Adjusting, closing, and reversing journal entries should be taught as part of the end-of-fiscal-period accounting procedures. The complexity of adjusting, closing, and reversing entries increases with the increased difficulty level of each cycle. Generally, reversing entries are taught toward the end of the first-year course or in the second-year course. The following activities comprise the elements which are essential to the understanding of recording adjusting, closing, and reversing entries.

Journalizing Adjusting Entries

At the end of a fiscal period, some account balances must be changed. Changes in account balances are referred to as adjustments. A work sheet was used to analyze and plan the adjusting entries (Chapter 7); however, the adjustment data from the work sheet must be recorded in a journal and posted to the ledger in order for the account balances to be updated.

Learning Outcomes. Students must know how to use the work sheet as the source document for the adjusting entries. In addition, students must be able to journalize and post the adjusting entries in an expanded or general journal.

Teaching Methods. Since all of the analysis connected with adjusting entries has been done in connection with the work sheet, concentrate on *why* the entries need to be recorded. *How* to record the entries is not new to students. After the financial statements have been prepared and analyzed, question students about the actual account balances. Lead the questions toward the understanding that until now the adjusting entries have been planned on the work sheet *only*. Until adjusting entries are journalized and posted, the account balances will *not* be accurate. Once students understand the need for making the journal entries, proceed to explain how the entries are actually recorded.

During the initial presentation about journalizing adjusting entries, each student should have access to a copy of a completed eight-column work sheet. Prepare and duplicate a completed work sheet, have students use one that was completed for an end-of-chapter problem, or have students look at an illustration of a work sheet in the textbook. Prepare a transparency of the journal to be used to record the adjusting entries and distribute a copy of a blank journal page to each student. Students should complete the journal along with the instructor.

Demonstrate how to use the information in the Adjustments columns of the worksheet to record an adjusting entry. Ask students to inspect the work sheet and decide what account should be debited in the first adjusting entry, the entry marked with the letter (a). When the correct account is determined, ask a student how to record the debit part of the entry in the journal. Since students have had previous experience at recording journal entries, recording an adjusting entry should be easy. Record the debit part of the entry and repeat the process for the credit part of the first entry. Stress that students do not need to re-analyze the adjusting entry. The analysis was done when the adjusting entries were planned and recorded on the work sheet. All that is necessary now is to journalize the entries.

Repeat the same procedure for the second adjusting entry labeled with the letter (b). Finally, students should journalize any remaining adjustments from the work sheet. When the remaining adjustments have been recorded, write the entries on the transparency so students can verify their work.

As an additional drill, refer students to another completed work sheet and have students individually record all adjusting entries. Project a transparency of the correct journal entries so that students' work can be verified.

Identifying Accounts That Need to be Closed

Revenue and expense information for a fiscal period is needed to figure net income for a business. Revenue and expense information is made available by recording all revenue and expenses for a fiscal period in temporary (nominal) accounts. Each temporary account must have a zero balance at the beginning of a new fiscal period. If the temporary accounts begin each period with zero balances, the ending balances in these accounts represent revenues and expenses *for that period only*! Once net income is calculated on the work sheet, the temporary accounts must be brought back to zero in order for the accounts to be ready to record revenue and expenses for the *next* period. Entries made to close temporary accounts to a zero balance are referred to as "closing entries."

Learning Outcomes. Students must be able to correctly identify which accounts need to be closed. To correctly identify the accounts which need to be closed, students must understand the purpose of closing entries. Students must also know that the work sheet is used as the source document for closing entries.

Teaching Methods. Introduce the topic of closing entries by discussing revenue accounts. Using a T account on the chalkboard or a transparency, illustrate a revenue account as of the end of a financial period. Stress that the account balance reflects revenues for the current period only. Ask students what would happen if the account was used to record revenues for the next accounting period. The desired answer is that the account balance would reflect revenues for both the current and prior accounting periods. Explain that the revenue for the current period would be difficult to determine; therefore, the revenue account balance must be decreased to zero at the end of the accounting period. If the account balance is decreased to zero, the account will be ready to record revenue for the next accounting period. At the end of the next accounting period, the revenue account will again reflect revenues for that accounting period *only*. The entry made to decrease the revenue account balance to zero is referred to as a "closing entry."

Follow the same procedure to illustrate why expense accounts and the drawing account must be closed at the end of each accounting period. Explain that revenue, expense, and the drawing accounts are called "temporary" accounts because the balance in these accounts is reduced to zero at the end of each period. On a transparency, display the Income Statement and Balance Sheet columns of a work sheet. Use the transparency to show that all temporary account balances are listed on the work sheet. The work sheet, therefore, is used as the source document for closing entries.

For extra practice, duplicate a drill similar to Illustration 8–1. Have students individually complete the drill. Students should answer "yes" or "no" to the question, "is Account Closed at End of Fiscal Period?" If the account is closed, students should indicate whether a debit or credit is necessary to close the account.

CLOSING ENTRIES

Account Title	Account Closed at End of Fiscal Period		Account Closed by	
	Yes	No	Debit	Credit
Cash				
Insurance Expense				
Income Summary				
Supplies Expense................				
Sales				
Prepaid Insurance				
Mary Larson, Capital				
Ace Enterprises (Liability) ...				
Advertising Expense				
Supplies				

Illustration 8–1 Drill on Identifying Accounts that Need to be Closed

Analyzing Closing Entries

A correct closing entry is one that transfers the account balance of one account to another account, causing the original account balance to equal zero. The common order of closing entries is (1) close revenue accounts, (2) close expense accounts, (3) close the income summary account and transfer the net income or net loss to the owner's capital account, and (4) close the drawing account.

Learning Outcomes. Students must be able to correctly analyze the information contained on the work sheet to determine the closing entries required to close the temporary accounts and prepare the ledger for the next fiscal period.

Teaching Methods. For the initial presentation of analyzing closing entries, have students refer to a work sheet previously completed in class or to an illustration of a work sheet in the textbook. State that the first closing entry is the entry to close the revenue account. During the first accounting cycle, only one revenue account is commonly used. Therefore, during the first presentation of closing entries, only one revenue account needs to be closed. Ask students to look at the completed work sheet and state the title and account balance of the revenue account. Write the information in T account form on the chalkboard as shown below:

```
              SALES
           |  Balance    1,200
           |
```

Ask what must be done to the Sales account to reduce the balance to zero—to "close" it. The desired answer is to debit the Sales account. Enter the debit in the T account as shown below:

```
              SALES
  Closing   1,200  |  Balance    1,200
                   |
```

Next, ask what must be done when one account is debited for $1,200.00. Students should answer that another account must be credited for the same amount. After obtaining the correct answer, display a T account on the chalkboard below the T account for sales. Label the T account "Income Summary" and enter a credit of $1,200.00 as shown below:

```
              SALES
  Closing   1,200  |  Balance    1,200
                   |

          INCOME SUMMARY
                   |  Closing    1,200
                   |
```

Teaching Recording of Adjusting, Closing and Reversing Entries

Explain that the Income Summary account is a temporary account used to summarize net income. Take time to review the purpose of closing entries. Remind students that a closing entry reduces the balance of a temporary account to zero and transfers the original balance to another account. Point out that the Sales account now has a zero balance and that the $1,200 balance from the Sales account has now been transferred to the Income Summary account. Stress that the Sales account originally had a credit balance and that the balance was transferred as a credit to the Income Summary account; therefore, the equality of debits and credits in the ledger has been maintained.

Follow the same procedure for analyzing and recording the second closing entry, the entry to close expense accounts. T accounts are shown below:

INSURANCE EXPENSE

Balance	400	Closing	400

SUPPLIES EXPENSE

Balance	150	Closing	150

UTILITIES EXPENSE

Balance	300	Closing	300

INCOME SUMMARY

Expenses	850	Revenue	1,200

Remind students that a closing entry reduces the balance of a temporary account to zero and transfers the original balance to another account. Point out that each expense account now has a zero balance and that the $850 total debit balances from the expense accounts have now been transferred to the Income Summary account. Point out that the expense accounts originally had debit balances and that the balances were transferred as a debit to the Income Summary account. Consequently, the equality of debits and credits in the ledger has been maintained.

State that the third closing entry closes the Income Summary account and transfers the net income or net loss to the owner's capital account. Place the Income Summary T account on the chalkboard. Remind students that the credit entry in Income Summary equals the revenue for the accounting period and that the debit entry in Income Summary equals the expenses for the accounting period. Ask students to calculate the balance in Income Summary. Explain that the balance in Income Summary is the same as the net income for the period, which is calculated by the formula "Revenue − Expenses = Net Income." Have students verify the balance by comparing their balance with the net income stated on the work sheet.

Follow the same procedure for analyzing and recording the third closing entry. T accounts are shown on page 94.

INCOME SUMMARY			
Expenses	850	Revenue	1,200
Closing	**350**		

TANIKA REYNOLDS, CAPITAL			
		Beg. Balance	6,500
		Net Income	**350**

Remind students that a closing entry reduces the balance of a temporary account to zero and transfers the original balance to another account. Explain that the Income Summary account now has a zero balance and that the net income or net loss from the Income Summary account has now been transferred to the owner's capital account. Point out that the income summary account originally had a credit balance and that the balance was transferred as a credit to the owner's equity account. Therefore, the equality of debits and credits in the ledger has been maintained. Ask students how net income affects owner's equity. The desired answer is that net income increases owner's equity. Point out that the net income has been added to the owner's capital account, thereby increasing owner's equity.

Follow the same procedure for analyzing and recording the fourth closing entry, the entry to close the drawing account. T accounts are shown below:

TANIKA REYNOLDS, CAPITAL			
Withdrawal	**150**	Beg. Balance	6,500
		Net Income	350

TANIKA REYNOLDS, DRAWING			
Balance	150	**Closing**	**150**

Remind students that a closing entry reduces the balance of a temporary account to zero and transfers the original balance to another account. Explain that the drawing account now has a zero balance and that the debit balance from the drawing account has now been transferred to the owner's capital account. Point out that the drawing account originally had a debit balance and that the balance was transferred as a debit to the owner's equity account. Therefore, the equality of debits and credits in the ledger has been maintained. Ask students how withdrawals affect owner's equity. The desired answer is that withdrawals decrease owner's equity. Point out that withdrawals have been recorded as a debit to the owner's capital account, thereby decreasing owner's equity.

All four closing entries have now been analyzed. To provide additional practice, give students another completed work sheet and have students use T accounts to analyze the required closing entries. When students are done, project the correct T accounts on a transparency.

To review the four closing entries, project another transparency similar to Illustration 8–2. The diagram in Illustration 8–2 could also be used as a bulletin board topic.

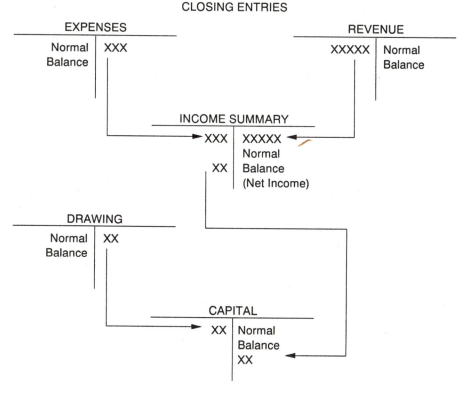

Illustration 8–2   Summary of Closing Entries

Journalizing Closing Entries

Although information needed to close the temporary accounts is contained on a work sheet, the closing entries must be recorded in a journal and posted to the ledger in order to actually close the accounts.

Learning Outcomes. Once the closing entries have been analyzed, students must be able to journalize and post the closing entries in an expanded or general journal.

Teaching Methods. Immediately after each closing entry is analyzed, ask how the entry would be recorded in a journal. Since students know how to journalize, they should be able to explain how to record the closing entry in the journal. Give each student a blank journal page. Record the correct entry on a transparency of a journal page and have students record the entry at the same time.

To provide additional practice after all four closing entries have been discussed, give students another completed work sheet and a blank journal page. Have students use T accounts to analyze the required closing entries and record the entries on the journal page. When students are done, project the correct T accounts and journal entries on a transparency.

Identifying Accounts that Need to be Reversed

In order to make future entries less complicated, some adjusting entries are reversed after the accounts are closed and the financial statements are prepared. If an adjusting entry creates an asset or liability account balance where none existed before, a reversing entry is recorded.

Learning Outcomes. Students must be able to correctly identify which accounts need to be reversed. To correctly identify which accounts need to be reversed, students must understand the purpose of reversing entries.

Teaching Methods. The best way to introduce the topic of reversing entries is to demonstrate the entries that are necessary if reversing entries are *not* made. Display on the chalkboard the following T accounts containing adjusting entries:

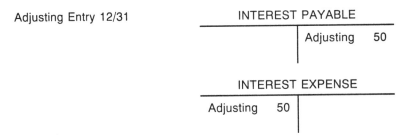

Remind students that the entry is necessary because the business has a note payable which is due in the next accounting period. The $50.00 interest expense represents the interest incurred on the note during the current accounting period. The note, together with the total interest, will be paid in the next accounting period.

Next, illustrate the balances in the two T accounts *after* closing entries have been recorded:

```
      Closing Entry 12/31              INTEREST PAYABLE
                                    ───────────────────────
                                    │  Adjusting    50

                                       INTEREST EXPENSE
                                    ───────────────────────
                                    Adjusting  50 │ Closing   50
```

Point out that the Interest Payable account is a permanent account and retains its balance. The Interest Expense account is a temporary account and is closed at the end of the accounting period.

Next, explain the entry that would be made when the note and interest are paid if a reversing entry is *not* made. Assume that the note was written on October 1 for

$500.00. Total interest on the note is $75.00. The note is due on February 1. Use T accounts to illustrate the entry:

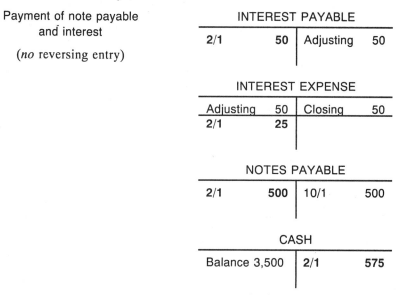

Payment of note payable and interest

(*no* reversing entry)

INTEREST PAYABLE			
2/1	50	Adjusting	50

INTEREST EXPENSE			
Adjusting	50	Closing	50
2/1	25		

NOTES PAYABLE			
2/1	500	10/1	500

CASH			
Balance 3,500		2/1	575

Explain the entry in detail. The liability, Interest Payable, is being paid and must be decreased. Interest Expense is debited to reflect the interest expense *for this period*, $25.00. The liability, Notes Payable, is being paid and must be decreased. Finally, the business must pay $575.00 for the note and the interest on the note.

Stress that the entry is complex. The accountant must remember that part of the interest was recorded during the last accounting period and that there is a balance in the Interest Payable account. The accountant could possibly forget that interest was recorded during the last accounting period and would, therefore, make an incorrect entry on February 1. To avoid having to remember this complex entry, a business may choose to make reversing entries. In a reversing entry, the adjusting entry is reversed.

Use T accounts to illustrate how a reversing entry would be recorded:

Reversing Entry 1/1

INTEREST PAYABLE			
1/1 Reversing	50	Adjusting	50

INTEREST EXPENSE			
Adjusting	50	Closing	50
		1/1 Reversing	50

Discuss the effect of the reversing entry. The liability account, Interest Payable, is reduced to a zero balance. The Interest Expense account has a credit balance. The benefit of the reversing entry will not be obvious until the entry for the payment of the note is illustrated. Use T accounts to illustrate the payment of the note and interest on February 1, as shown on page 98.

Payment of note payable
and interest

(*with* reversing entry)

INTEREST EXPENSE			
Adjusting	50	Closing	50
2/1	75	1/1 Reversing	50

NOTES PAYABLE			
2/1	500	10/1	500

CASH			
Balance	3,500	2/1	575

Point out that the balance in every account is exactly the same as it was after the payment of the note when a reversing entry was *not* done. The Interest Expense account balance, $25.00, reflects the interest *for this period*. The liability, Notes Payable, is being paid and is reduced to a zero balance. Cash is decreased by the total amount paid for the note and the interest, $575.00.

Stress that the benefit of the reversing entry is the simplicity of the entry to record payment, which does not require the accountant to remember what adjusting entries were made.

Review the rule for reversing entries. If an adjusting entry creates an asset or liability account balance where none existed before, a reversing entry is recorded. (One exception to the reversing rule is the adjusting entry for Income Tax Payable, which is usually not reversed.) Use flash cards to give students practice on which adjusting entries are reversed. Prepare flash cards showing one adjusting entry on the front of each card. Ask all students to respond "reverse" or "do not reverse" for each card. For a variation of the drill, call on an individual student to respond.

Finally, give students a list of adjusting entries. Ask students to prepare reversing entries for those adjusting entries which require reversing. Upon completion, project the correct reversing entries on a transparency.

Journalizing Reversing Entries

The adjusting entries to be reversed must be recorded in a journal and posted. Adjusting entries that are reversed are referred to as "reversing entries."

Learning Outcomes. Once the reversing entries have been identified, students must be able to journalize and post the reversing entries in an expanded or general journal.

Teaching Methods. Since a reversing entry is the reverse of the adjusting entry, no analysis is necessary. Immediately after each reversing entry is identified, ask how the entry would be recorded in a journal. Since students know the adjusting entry, they should be able to explain how to record the reversing entry in the journal. Give each student a blank journal page. Record the correct entry on a transparency of a journal page and have students record the entry at the same time.

To provide additional practice, give students a journal page containing adjusting entries. Have students record the required reversing entries on the bottom of the journal page. When students are done, project the correct journal entries on a transparency.

GENERAL CONSIDERATIONS

Since students know how to journalize entries, the adjusting and reversing entries should present no problems. Instead, concentrate on the reasons for recording adjusting and reversing entries.

Closing entries will require analysis. Students who understand w*hy* closing entries are made, will find it easier to remember *how* the entries are made.

CHAPTER 9
INTEGRATING COMPUTERS INTO ACCOUNTING INSTRUCTION

The integration of computers into the accounting curriculum is no longer a topic of debate. Technological advancements have reduced computer costs and increased computer capabilities. Consequently, computers are being used to process accounting data in both large and small businesses. In order to equip accounting students with the skills necessary for entry-level accounting positions, the accounting curriculum must include experience in automated accounting.

Automated accounting does not change basic accounting concepts, principles, and procedures as the same accounting cycle applies to both manual and automated accounting. A computer is used in automated accounting to perform the routine and repetitive steps in the accounting cycle. Manual methods are used in automated accounting to capture, arrange, and input accounting data into a computer and to interpret accounting information prepared by a computer. Whether manual or automated procedures are used, the accountant is still in control and must determine if the correct procedures are being applied.

This chapter will not discuss the learning outcomes or the teaching methods necessary for automated accounting as they are similar to the learning outcomes and teaching methods discussed for manual accounting instruction. Instead, this chapter will discuss alternative methods for integrating computerized accounting into the normal high school accounting curriculum, types of software available, how to select software, and how to set up and operate an automated accounting classroom.

THREE MAJOR APPROACHES TO INTEGRATING COMPUTERS INTO ACCOUNTING INSTRUCTION

There are three major approaches to integrating computers into the accounting curriculum. All three approaches, however, agree that automated accounting should not be introduced until students have mastered the first complete accounting cycle for a service business. Students learn automated accounting best when this new learning builds on the knowledge, understanding, and application gained from working through the same procedures manually. No new accounting theory should be covered during automated accounting activities. Rather, introduce the computer as a tool to solve problems students already know.

As discussed later, the availability of equipment and/or the software program chosen may determine which approach is taken. All three approaches should be carefully considered to determine which approach most closely fits the instructor's philosophy.

Integrating Computers With a Stand-Alone Unit

After students have mastered the complete accounting cycle for a service business, a complete automated cycle could be covered emphasizing another service business. Using a stand-alone unit will give students the opportunity to work through a second entire accounting cycle for a service business. Students can concentrate on applying computer procedures to an already-familiar accounting cycle.

Integrating Computers Within Cycles

As students progress through advanced accounting cycles, related computer applications can be completed. For example, as students learn the accounting cycle for a partnership, a computer application covering recording and posting of partnership transactions could be completed. Once through the accounting cycle for a partnership, students could complete another computer application covering end-of-fiscal-period work for a partnership.

Integrating Computers at the End of Cycles

After students have mastered any accounting cycle manually, an automated version of a reinforcement activity and/or a business simulation could be completed. These activities would reinforce the entire manual cycle while allowing students to see how computers can assist in the repetitive tasks of accounting.

TYPES OF EDUCATIONAL SOFTWARE

Various types of educational software are available for use in the accounting curriculum. Most publishing companies offer several types of software designed to fit the objectives of a variety of accounting courses.

Application Problems

Application problems are usually designed to fit one of the integration approaches discussed at the beginning of this chapter. If the second approach is being followed, the application problems will most likely consist of shorter applications of the accounting cycle recently covered. If the first or third approach is being followed, the application problems will most likely consist of a series of steps covering the entire accounting cycle.

Textbook Problems. Many textbooks have end-of-chapter problems that are designed to be done both manually and on a computer. Students should complete the problem manually before attempting to complete the problem on the computer. These problems provide students the opportunity to compare the results obtained from a manual accounting system with the results obtained from a computerized accounting system.

Supplemental Problems. In addition to the textbook problems, publishers also provide supplemental problems designed to be completed on the computer. Since students are not doing the supplemental problems manually, there is no opportunity to compare procedures and results under the two systems. Supplemental problems do give students the opportunity to complete more computerized problems to reinforce automated applications.

Simulations/Practice Sets

Computerized simulations (practice sets) cover a wide range of integration possibilities. Some simulations are designed to be done manually and/or on the computer, which allows much flexibility as to how the simulations are integrated into the accounting course. Other computerized simulations are not designed to be completed manually. Computerized simulations are available for service businesses, merchandising businesses, and manufacturing businesses. While all simulations require knowledge of the entire accounting cycle, the time required to complete the simulations varies depending on the number of transactions included and the degree of detail the simulation includes. For example, some simulations require students to produce checks while other simulations only require cash payment entries to be made.

Some simulations include subsidiary ledgers, inventory procedures, payroll, and separate subsystems for cash payments, cash receipts, sales of merchandise, purchases, and general accounting. Subsystems should be integrated with other subsystems in the simulations. For example, in some simulations a sale of merchandise automatically reduces the inventory of the item sold. This is referred to as an integrated subsystem approach. Other simulations would require the sale of merchandise transaction to be entered into both the sales subsystem and the inventory subsystem.

Computerized simulations also vary in the amount of technical computer knowledge required to operate the accounting program.

Related Programs

Non-accounting programs are also appropriate for the accounting curriculum. Two major kinds of programs are electronic spreadsheets and payroll programs. Programs such as spreadsheets and payroll do not concentrate on transaction analysis, accounting entries, or posting. Instead, related programs assist in producing financial reports such as income statements, balance sheets, and payroll registers. Related programs are typically not used in the first presentation of the accounting cycle.

Spreadsheets. Electronic spreadsheet programs can be integrated into the accounting curriculum at various levels. While electronic spreadsheet programs do not reinforce the entire accounting cycle, specific concepts are reinforced. For example, the spreadsheet problem may include the use of comparative income statements on which component percentages are to be calculated and analyzed. These programs reduce the amount of time required to perform repetitive mathematical functions and allow students to spend more time on the analysis of the results.

Electronic spreadsheet programs are usually integrated into the accounting curriculum after at least one accounting cycle has been covered. A major disadvantage of electronic spreadsheet programs is that students must learn the spreadsheet commands before being able to apply accounting concepts. In some cases, the command structure is complex and requires several hours of instruction before students are able to comfortably operate the program.

Some publishers provide supplemental spreadsheet problems which either correlate with or complement the textbook problems.

Payroll. Computerized payroll programs can also be integrated into the accounting curriculum. Typically, payroll programs are "stand alone" programs, which means that they cover only payroll functions. Such a program can be used to reinforce the payroll concepts covered in the normal accounting curriculum. However, most payroll programs do not include the accounting entries associated with payroll. Many payroll programs allow the user to use pre-existing problems or to input payroll problems developed by the instructor.

CHOOSING SOFTWARE

Many factors must be considered before a software program is chosen for use in the accounting course. The decision is somewhat complicated by the large variety of programs available; however, this variety allows more flexibility in integrating computers into the accounting curriculum. Regardless of the goals of the course or what restrictions there are on hardware accessibility, programs can be found to match these goals and restrictions.

The instructor should model good ethics by using only legally-obtained software. Many vendors offer a site license which permits a school to make multiple copies of the program for use on site. Software programs which require data to be entered only once and which incorporate the data into all related subsystems, such as general ledger, accounts receivable, and accounts payable, are referred to as integrated software. Integrated software is preferable, since it is used in most business settings.

Assess Hardware Availability

If the hardware is already in place, the program selection will be limited to programs that will operate on that hardware. The accessibility of the hardware also needs to be considered. Some questions that must be considered are:

1. How many computers are available for accounting instruction?
2. How many hours of the day are the computers available?
3. Do the available hours coincide with the scheduled accounting course(s)?
4. Are the computers in the accounting classroom or are they in a separate room or lab? Will the instructor be in the same room while the students are working on the computer?
5. What type of computer is available? How much memory does each computer have?
6. How many disk drives are available for each computer? Are hard drives available?
7. Is a network available?
8. Are printers available? How many? What type? What size?

If the hardware is to be purchased to match the program selected, the above questions still need to be anticipated. The software purchased must be adaptable to the hardware availability and physical location.

Develop Goals and Philosophy

Once the hardware restrictions are known, the goals and philosophy of the accounting course must be developed in line with the hardware restrictions. Questions to consider during the development of the course goals include:

1. What is the purpose of integrating computers into the accounting course? What is hoped to be accomplished?
2. Will students only be exposed to computerized accounting? Are students expected to become proficient at computerized accounting?
3. Which approach for integrating computers into the accounting curriculum best fits the availability of equipment and the goals of the program?
4. What types of programs will be integrated? Application problems? Simulations/practice sets? Related programs?
5. Given the number of computers available, will all students work on computers at the same time or will students be rotated on and off the computers?
6. How much time can be devoted to computer applications?
7. Will the computers be used by all students? Only by advanced (2d year) students? Only by higher-level beginning students?

Educational Software vs. Commercial Software

Closely related to the goals and philosophy of the course is the decision to use educational software or to use commercial software. Each type has its advantages.

Commercial accounting programs offer the following advantages:

1. higher level of sophistication, more powerful, faster;
2. more integration of subsystems;
3. inventory, payroll, subsidiary subsystems are more available;
4. better error checking and error correction features;
5. ability to use instructor-prepared problems; and
6. better transfer to programs used in business.

Educational accounting programs offer the following advantages:

1. designed for students with reinforcement drills, etc.;
2. instructions written for student learners;
3. new learning presented in step-by-step format;
4. better documentation;
5. already prepared problems;
6. pre-designed input forms;
7. teacher guides, solution manuals, tests, answer keys, transparencies; and
8. lower price.

The choice between commercial and educational accounting programs should be dependent on the goals of the accounting course, the money available, the amount of teacher-preparation time available, and the amount of support available from the publisher or producer.

In all but a few situations, educational accounting software programs fit the requirements and restrictions of a high-school level accounting course. The major disadvantage of the commercial programs is the lack of structured problems. If a commercial program is used, all problems and all support materials need to be prepared by the instructor.

Compare and Evaluate Software

The most time-consuming aspect of software selection is comparing and evaluating the software. By this step, however, many programs will have been eliminated due to hardware availability and the goals of the accounting course. Those programs still being considered need to be compared and evaluated. The best way to accomplish this evaluation is to actually work through the programs following the same directions that students would follow. If the programs are not available for personal evaluation, the features can be compared by talking to company representatives and/or instructors who use the various programs.

Some important features to compare include:

1. Student instructions—are instructions clear, correct, and easy to follow? Can students follow the directions without teacher assistance? (Clear instructions are especially important if one or two students will be going to another room to use the computers.)
2. Input forms—are forms accurate, complete, and set up for efficient input of data?
3. Chart of accounts—can accounts be added, deleted, or changed easily?
4. Journal entry—does the program allow the entire entry to be visible on the screen? Can corrections be made immediately?
5. Equality of debits and credits—does the program automatically check each transaction for equality of debits and credits?
6. Error checks—does the program check for obviously incorrect data such as account numbers not on the chart of accounts?
7. Error correction—does the program allow for the correction of entry errors? Is the correction feature easy to use?
8. Ledger accounts—can the activity in each ledger account be viewed or are only balances available?
9. Reports—what reports are available? Can reports be viewed on the screen as well as printed on paper?
10. Ease of operation—can the program be operated with a minimum amount of computer experience and/or training? Can students run the program with a minimum amount of effort going to computer operations?
11. Subsystems—are subsidiary ledgers and other subsystems integrated with the general journal program and with each other?
12. Methods—are the methods and procedures compatible with the methods and procedures used in the text? Are acceptable accounting methods followed? Are financial reports produced in an acceptable form?
13. Program disks—is the program disk used only to drive the program or is student data stored on it? If student data is stored on the program disk, is a separate program disk required for each student, each class period? If student

data is stored on a separate disk, can the same program disk be used by students in different class periods?
14. Support system—is telephone computer support available? Is the hotline service free of charge?

LOGISTICS

When computer usage is integrated into the accounting curriculum, it usually means that the computers must be incorporated into the classroom. Even if the computers are in another room, the hardware must be configured and arranged to promote efficient operation. Finally, the management of students needs to be considered and pre-arranged.

Classroom Set Up

The number of computers and the size of the room will limit the number of classroom layout options available. One successful layout is to have all computers against the perimeter walls, with student work tables or desks in the center of the classroom. This layout allows the instructor to view all computers from one location and provides for work stations away from the computers. These work stations can be used for preparing input forms, giving group instructions, and conducting group discussions.

Although the layout described above is successful, several factors must be considered in determining the optimal layout for the classroom. Electrical outlets must be available. The computer monitors must be located so that the screen is free of glare from sunlight or artificial lights. Curtains or window shades may be necessary to prevent glare. Student work stations should be available for the preparation of input forms, the verification of totals, and the analysis of results.

Thought must be given to the security and protection of the hardware and software. If the school does not have a good security system, an alarm system may need to be installed in the computer room. Precautions must be taken against static build up. Locking cabinets should be available for software storage. Unless the system is networked, a check-out system for software must be established and implemented.

Hardware Configuration

The accounting program chosen will determine the amount of hardware required. If the program allows viewing financial reports on the screen, fewer printers are necessary than if all reports must be printed. For most situations, one printer for each computer is not necessary. Two or three computers per printer is generally adequate. If computers will be sharing a printer, a switch box should be used to switch from one computer to another, eliminating the need to continually connect and disconnect the computer cables and the printer.

As accounting programs become more powerful, the operation of the program will more likely require a hard drive or two disk drives per computer. Hard drives or double disk drives are especially important for programs that store student data on personal data disks rather than storing student data on the program disk.

Group Vs. Individual Work

The decision to have students work individually or in groups will be influenced both by the instructor's educational philosophy and the availability of the hardware. Many options exist.

The input forms can be prepared together as a class, in small groups, or on an individual basis. A combination of methods may also be used. The first time input forms are used, the class can prepare the forms together, discussing how and why the forms are used. By preparing the forms as a class, the accuracy of the initial computer input can be increased. Students can focus on how to input the data into the computer. As students become more experienced, input forms can be prepared in groups of two. Eventually, students may be required to prepare input forms individually.

If the number of computers does not allow one computer per student, groups of two may be formed. When groups of two are used, one student can read the input forms aloud while the other group member keys the data into the computer. Students should change places throughout the problem so that both students have the opportunity to key the data into the computer. Groups of two allow students to work cooperatively, discussing and clarifying procedures for each other. Normally, groups larger than two are not successful.

Whether working individually or in groups, students should be taught to complete all input forms *before* sitting at the computer. Computer time is valuable and students should be made aware of ways to use the hardware efficiently.

When hardware and/or time restrictions do not allow all students to work on the computers at the same time, the instructor needs to determine who uses the computer first. One solution is to have the better students go first, allowing more students to use the equipment in the smallest amount of time. Another solution is to pair a higher-ability student with a lower-ability student. Pairing high-and-low ability together provides the extra help that the low-ability student may need.

INSTRUCTOR'S ROLE

Once the program has been purchased, the equipment has been arranged, and numerous teaching decisions have been made, introduce students to the program. Explain the purpose and use of input forms. Display transparencies of the reports that will be printed. Explain the necessity of following directions carefully. The instructor's role will then become one of facilitator. As students complete activities, discuss the parallel manual procedure. Students must understand that they are following the same accounting procedures that they followed manually. This will encourage students to think about what they are doing and make them aware of the benefits of automated accounting.

Remind students that even though the computer is doing the calculating, the computer operator is still responsible for the accuracy of the results. Encourage students to verify totals generated by the computer and to check the financial reports to determine if the results are reasonable.

EVALUATION

Evaluating student performance on computerized accounting activities is similar to evaluating student performance on manual accounting activities. Measurement and evaluation procedures are covered in Chapter 11.

GENERAL CONSIDERATIONS

Automated accounting can be integrated into any accounting course, regardless of equipment or time constraints. Students may only be able to complete two or three problems on the computer. Students will encounter automated accounting in entry-level accounting positions. Therefore, accounting students need a basic understanding of computers and how they may be used in automated accounting. Students need not become proficient in the highly technical aspects of computer operation and programming.

Viewing an automated accounting system in operation will help students realize the importance of computers in accounting. Such a field trip could be taken either before or after students have actually worked on the computers.

On a bulletin board, display the input forms used in the program and the reports generated by the program. The bulletin board can serve as an introduction to automated accounting and as a summary of automated accounting activities.

Model ethical behavior by using only legally-obtained software. Discuss how copyright laws apply to computer software and when legal copies of software can be made. A guest speaker could be used to explain how compliance with copyright laws is monitored in the work place.

CHAPTER **10**

TEACHING ACCOUNTING CONTROL SYSTEMS: PAYROLL, VOUCHERS, AND INVENTORY

The principal purpose for keeping accounting records is to provide financial information to business managers and owners. Accounting records are also used to help protect the resources of a business by controlling the way assets are used and kept. Special accounting systems are designed to help control specific types and uses of assets. Three common special control systems are (1) payroll, (2) vouchers, and (3) inventory.

ESSENTIAL ELEMENTS OF ACCOUNTING CONTROL SYSTEMS

Special control systems generally included in a first-year accounting course are (1) payroll and (2) vouchers. The special control system for inventory is generally included in a second-year accounting course. The following activities comprise the elements which are essential to the understanding of the payroll, voucher, and inventory control systems.

Payroll System

A payroll system affects all employees of a business and must provide information needed to prepare reports for federal and state agencies. Therefore, information must be recorded to meet the requirements of the business' accounting system, the employees, and the government reports.

Calculating Earnings From a Time Card. A payroll time card is generally used daily to record the time an employee begins and stops work. At the end of a pay period, the total time recorded on the time card is calculated and the employee earnings for the pay period are calculated. The following steps are used to figure employee earnings:

1. Calculate each day's regular and overtime hours worked.
2. Calculate regular earnings (regular hours × regular pay rate).
3. Calculate overtime earnings (overtime hours × overtime pay rate).
4. Calculate total earnings (regular earnings + overtime earnings).

1. Learning Outcomes. Students must be able to calculate the number of regular and overtime hours worked during a pay period. Using the hours worked and the hourly rate of pay, the total earnings for a pay period can be calculated.

2. Teaching Methods. Using a transparency of a time card similar to the completed time card in Illustration 10-1, calculate and record the hours worked for two days. Ask questions leading to the conclusion that time is generally recorded in the nearest 1/4 hour segments. Also establish that definitions for overtime may vary,

	MORNING		AFTERNOON		OVERTIME		HOURS	
	IN	OUT	IN	OUT	IN	OUT	REG	OT
1	7:58	12:02	12:58	5:05			8	
2	7:58	12:03	12:59	5:02	5:58	8:01	8	2
3	8:04	12:01	12:56	5:01			8	
4	7:57	12:00	12:53	5:04	6:01	6:59	8	1
5	7:59	12:02	12:58	5:01			8	
8	7:59	12:00	12:59	5:02			8	
9	7:57	12:02	12:55	5:02			8	
10	7:56	12:02	12:59	5:03	5:59	7:00	8	1
11	7:58	12:01	12:56	5:03			8	
12	7:55	12:02	12:57	5:02			8	

EMPLOYEE NO. 1
NAME Tawnya Field
PERIOD ENDING April 15, 19—

	HOURS	RATE	AMOUNT
REGULAR	80	6.20	496.00
OVERTIME	4	9.30	37.20
TOTAL HOURS	84	TOTAL EARNINGS	533.20

Illustration 10-1 Time Card Showing Total Hours Worked and Total Earnings

but generally more than 40 hours per week and 8 hours per day are classified as overtime. Overtime pay rates usually are 1 1/2 times regular rates but may vary from business to business. Personal work experiences of students can contribute to the discussion. Have students individually calculate the hours worked for the remaining days. Call on students for their solutions and write correct responses on the transparency.

Explain how to calculate and record regular earnings, overtime earnings, and total earnings.

To provide additional practice for students, display a transparency with exercises similar to Illustration 10–2. Reveal one exercise at a time, asking students to calculate the regular, overtime, and total earnings. Solicit answers from students and record correct amounts on the transparency.

Employee Number	Hours Worked		Pay Rate	Amount of Pay		Total Earnings
	Regular	Overtime		Regular	Overtime	
1	40	2	$4.60			
2	38	0	5.80			
3	40	4	7.00			
4	40	1	6.50			
5	40	5	7.50			

Illustration 10–2   Drill on Calculating Regular, Overtime, and Total Earnings

Preparing a Payroll Register.   A payroll register is used to record earnings, deductions, and net pay for all employees for one pay period. A payroll register is the source document for payroll transactions.

1. Learning Outcomes.   Students must be able to correctly prepare a payroll register. To prepare a payroll register, students must (a) record regular and overtime earnings from time cards, (b) determine income and FICA tax deductions, and (c) calculate net pay.

2. Teaching Methods.   Distribute a handout and display a transparency with payroll information on the top and a blank payroll register on the bottom. Illustration 10–3 shows a completed version of the transparency. Explain that information for the payroll register is usually obtained from employee time cards and W-4 forms, which show marital status and number of withholding allowances. Demonstrate how to record information regarding Employee No. 1. On the transparency, write in employee number, name, marital status, number of allowances, regular earnings, overtime earnings, and total earnings.

Ask students what factors affect the amount of income tax withheld. The desired answer is total earnings, marital status, number of withholding allowances, and the pay period. Refer students to an income tax withholding table in the textbook. Ask students how much income tax should be withheld for Employee No. 1. Record the correct answer in the Federal Income Tax column.

On the chalkboard, show students how to calculate FICA tax by using a given percentage, such as 8%, or the current FICA tax rate. Record the amount of FICA tax to be withheld for Employee No. 1 in the FICA Tax column.

Employee		Mar. Status	No. of Allow.	Earnings		Deductions	
No.	Name			Regular	Overtime	Insurance	Bonds
1	Tawnya Field	S	1	$496.00	$37.20	$37.00	$10.00
2	Randy Larson	M	4	520.00	19.50		10.00
3	Brent Kahls	S	1	388.00		37.00	
4	Jason Yurik	M	3	544.00	30.60	45.00	
5	Brenda Putnum	M	2	448.00			10.00

PAYROLL REGISTER

SEMIMONTHLY PERIOD ENDED April 15, 19—   DATE OF PAYMENT April 16, 19—

EMPL. NO.	EMPLOYEE'S NAME	MARITAL STATUS	NO. OF ALLOWANCES	EARNINGS			FEDERAL INCOME TAX	FICA TAX	DEDUCTIONS			TOTAL	NET PAY	CHECK NO.
				REGULAR	OVERTIME	TOTAL			HEALTH INSURANCE	OTHER				
1	Tawnya Field	S	1	496 00	37 20	533 20	61 00	42 66	37 00	(B) 10 00		150 66	382 54	1
2	Randy Larson	M	4	520 00	19 50	539 50	12 00	43 16		(B) 10 00		65 16	474 34	2
3	Brent Kahls	S	1	388 00		388 00	39 00	31 04	37 00			107 04	280 96	3
4	Jason Yurik	M	3	544 00	30 60	574 60	30 00	45 97	45 00			120 97	453 63	4
5	Brenda Putnum	M	2	448 00		448 00	23 00	35 84		(B) 10 00		68 84	379 16	5
				2396 00	87 30	2483 30	165 00	198 67	119 00	30 00		512 67	1970 63	

Illustration 10–3   Totaled and Ruled Payroll Register

Explain that total deductions is the sum of all amounts deducted from Employee No. 1's total earnings. Add the deductions on line 1 and enter the total in the Total Deductions column. Ask students how net pay is calculated. Most likely, students will answer with the formula:

Total Earnings − Total Deductions = Net Pay

Calculate the net pay for Employee No. 1 and record the amount in the Net Pay column.

Have students complete line 2 of the payroll register, calculating net pay for Employee No. 2. Call on individual students to obtain the amounts calculated for each column. Record correct answers on the transparency. Have students figure the amounts for the remaining employees. When students have finished, check their work for accuracy.

Demonstrate how to check the accuracy of totals on the payroll register. (Total of Total Earnings column minus total of Total Deductions column equals total of Net Pay column.)

If students have previously ruled journals, ask how the payroll register should be ruled. Using previous knowledge, students should be able to explain the ruling procedure. Demonstrate correct totaling and ruling on the transparency.

Preparing an Employee's Earnings Record. A separate employee earnings record is used to record earnings, deductions, net pay, and accumulated earnings for each employee for the year. An employee earnings record is the source of information for required reports that must be prepared by the business.

1. Learning Outcomes. Students must be able to record the earnings, deductions, and net pay from the payroll register into the employee earnings record. In addition, students must be able to calculate accumulated earnings for the year.

2. Teaching Methods. Distribute a blank employee earnings record and a page of additional data similar to that given in Illustration 10–4. Display a transparency of a blank employee earnings record.

ADDITIONAL EMPLOYEE DATA

Name: Tawnya Field
Rate of Pay: $6.20
Social Security No.: 423-76-1379
Position: Delivery Driver
Accum. Earnings for 1st Qtr.: $3,278.00

Illustration 10–4 Additional Data Needed for Employee Earnings Record

Using the payroll register and the additional employee data, complete the heading on the employee earnings record. Demonstrate how payroll information is transferred from the payroll register to the employee earnings record. Explain how to calculate the new Accumulated Earnings and that accumulated earnings is needed for tax purposes. Ask students to calculate the new total for accumulated earnings and record the correct amount in the appropriate column. A completed employee earnings record is given in Illustration 10–5.

EARNINGS RECORD FOR QUARTER ENDED

EMPLOYEE NO. __1__

LAST NAME __FIELD__ FIRST __TAWNYA__ MIDDLE INITIAL ____ MARITAL STATUS __S__ WITHHOLDING ALLOWANCES __1__

RATE OF PAY __6.20__ PER HR. SOCIAL SECURITY NO. __423-76-1379__ POSITION __DELIVERY DRIVER__

PAY PERIOD		EARNINGS			DEDUCTIONS					ACCUMULATED EARNINGS
NO.	ENDED	REGULAR	OVERTIME	TOTAL	FEDERAL INCOME TAX	FICA TAX	HEALTH INSURANCE	OTHER	TOTAL	NET PAY	
		1	2	3	4	5	6	7	8	9	10
											3278 00
1	4-15	496 00	37 20	533 20	61 00	42 66	37 00 (B)	10 00	150 66	382 54	3811 20
2											
3											
4											
5											
6											
7											
QUARTERLY TOTALS											

OTHER DEDUCTIONS: B—U.S. SAVINGS BONDS; UW—UNITED WAY

Illustration 10-5 Employee Earnings Record

Explain that a separate employee earnings record is used to keep payroll information about each employee for all pay periods. Payroll information for individual employees is necessary for reports to the employee and to the government.

Analyzing, Journalizing, and Posting Payroll Transactions and Employer Payroll Taxes. Although other payroll records are prepared, all transactions associated with a payroll must be journalized and posted so that payroll transactions will be included in general ledger accounts.

1. Learning Outcomes. Students must be able to correctly calculate and record all transactions associated with a payroll. The transactions include (a) making a journal entry for a payroll transaction, (b) calculating and making a journal entry for the employer payroll taxes, (c) making a journal entry for payment of withholding and payroll tax liabilities, and (d) posting these payroll entries to the appropriate general ledger accounts.

2. Teaching Methods. Display a transparency of the completed payroll register. On the chalkboard, draw T accounts for Salary Expense, Employee Income Tax Payable, FICA Tax Payable, Health Insurance Premium Payable, U.S. Savings Bonds Payable, and Cash. Explain that the payroll transaction needs to be recorded in the journal so that the amounts will be included in the general ledger accounts.

Ask questions that will assist students in analyzing the payroll transaction. As correct answers are given, record the debit and credits in the T accounts as follows:

SALARY EXPENSE		EMPLOYEE INCOME TAX PAY.	
4-16 2483.30			4-16 165.00

FICA TAX PAYABLE		HEALTH INSURANCE PREM. PAY.	
	4-16 198.67		4-16 119.00

U.S. SAVINGS BONDS PAY.		CASH	
	4-16 30.00		4-16 1970.63

Distribute a blank journal page to each student. Tell students to use the T accounts on the chalkboard to record the payroll transaction in the journal. When students are done, display the correct journal entry on a transparency so students can verify their work.

Similar procedures should be followed to teach the journal entry for payroll taxes expense. Display the completed payroll register again as a basis for analyzing and preparing a journal entry for payroll taxes expense. On the chalkboard, draw T accounts for Payroll Taxes Expense, FICA Tax Payable, Unemploy. Tax Pay. — Fed., and Unemploy. Tax Pay. — State.

Remind students that the employer must pay the same rate of FICA tax for the employees as is withheld from each employee's earnings. Discuss the employer's responsibility to pay unemployment taxes to both the federal and state government.

Teaching Accounting Control Systems: Payroll, Vouchers, and Inventory

Tell students to use the unemployment tax rate given in the textbook. Current rates at the time of this publication are federal unemployment, 0.8%; state unemployment, 5.4%. Both unemployment taxes are paid on each employee's first $7,000.00 of earnings per year. Since none of the employees in the example have earned $7,000.00, unemployment taxes will be paid on total earnings.

Ask questions that will assist students in analyzing the payroll tax expense transaction. As correct answers are given, record the debit and credits in the T accounts as follows:

PAYROLL TAXES EXPENSE		FICA TAX PAYABLE	
4-16 352.64			4-16 198.67

UNEMPLOY. TAX PAY.—FED		UNEMPLOY. TAX PAY.—STATE	
	4-16 19.87		4-16 134.10

Using the same journal page used for the payroll transaction, tell students to use the T accounts on the chalkboard to record the payroll transaction in the journal. When students are done, display the correct journal entry on a transparency so students can verify their work.

Voucher System

Cash is more often subject to misuse than other assets because ownership is so easy to transfer. A voucher system is used by some businesses to increase control of cash payments. Entry level accounting employees frequently perform tasks relating to some part of a voucher system.

Preparing and Recording a Voucher in a Voucher Register. A voucher is a business form used to show an authorized person's approval for a cash payment. Vouchers are recorded in a voucher register, which serves as a journal and replaces the purchases and cash payments journals.

1. Learning Outcomes. Students must be able to accurately prepare and record a voucher in a voucher register. Preparing a voucher includes (a) verifying an invoice, and (b) preparing a voucher to include accounts and amounts to be debited and credited. Recording a voucher includes transferring the information from the voucher to the voucher register.

2. Teaching Methods. Before presenting the entries required in a voucher system, discuss what a voucher system is and why a voucher system should be used. If some students have had work experience with a voucher system, have those students describe their experiences with vouchers. Invite a guest speaker from a local business that uses vouchers to describe the system used. Emphasize that a voucher system is a control procedure that requires all cash payments to be approved by someone in authority and that the voucher register serves as a journal and replaces the purchases and cash payments journals.

Have a team of students secure a set of forms used in the voucher system of a local business. These forms can be displayed on a bulletin board to illustrate the step-by-step procedures used to process a transaction through a voucher system. Reference the bulletin board throughout the study of vouchers.

To explain how a voucher is prepared, display a blank voucher form on a transparency. Using a textbook example, complete the voucher and explain the purpose for including each item. Remind students that, when using a voucher system, one voucher must be completed for each cash payment.

Distribute a blank voucher form to each student. Again, using a textbook example, have students complete the voucher. Verify student work by displaying a correct voucher on a transparency.

Distribute a handout listing several transactions to be entered in a voucher register. Analyze the first transaction. On the chalkboard, prepare the journal entry as it would appear in a purchases, cash payments, or a multi-column journal—whichever is appropriate.

Next, enter the same transaction on a transparency of a voucher register. Ask one or two students to explain any differences in the two entries. The desired answer is that the account Vouchers Payable is always credited for the transaction amount in a voucher register. In a purchases, cash payments, or multi-column journal, either accounts payable or cash is credited. Answer all questions relating to the entry. Distribute a blank voucher register to each student. Ask students to prepare the voucher register entry for the second transaction on the handout. Record and display the correct entry on the transparency. Discuss the similarities and differences between using a voucher register and using other journals. Have students complete the remaining transactions. When students are done, display a transparency of the completed voucher register and ask students to verify their work.

Remind students that every voucher must be recorded in a voucher register and that all voucher numbers must be accounted for.

Recording Cash Payments in a Check Register. A check register is a journal used in a voucher system to record cash payments. A check register is similar to and replaces a cash payments journal.

1. Learning Outcomes. Students must be able to accurately record a cash payment in a check register. Recording a cash payment in a check register includes (a) maintaining bank balance columns in a check register, (b) recording checks in a check register, and (c) posting from a check register.

2. Teaching Methods. On a transparency of a check register, enter the "balance on hand" notation on the first line. Point out the similarities between the check register and the check stub of a checkbook. Demonstrate how to record payment of the first voucher entered on the voucher register used in the previous drill. Next, illustrate posting the date and check number to the voucher register.

Distribute a handout containing cash payment transactions and cash deposits related to the transactions in the completed voucher register. Have students record the next cash payment transaction. Ask two or three students to give their check register entries. Record the correct entry on the check register transparency. Follow the same procedure as students record two or three check register entries. Next, have students complete entries for the remaining transactions. Randomly select students to give their check register entries. Display the completed check register on a transparency and ask students to verify their work.

Finally, remind students that all cash payments must be supported by an authorized voucher. When the voucher is paid, the payment must be recorded in the check register.

Inventory System

A business must keep accurate records of inventory on hand. The amount of inventory on hand is used to calculate cost of merchandise sold and, therefore, affects the amount of net income the business reports for the fiscal period. An inventory system must accurately record and report inventory on hand.

Determining the Cost of Merchandise Inventory. In a periodic inventory system, increases and decreases in inventory are not recorded in the merchandise inventory account when merchandise is purchased and sold. During the accounting period, therefore, the merchandise inventory account balance is equal to the beginning balance in the account. At the end of the accounting period, the amount of merchandise remaining in inventory is counted. After inventory is counted, a dollar amount must be attached to the cost of the inventory. A business must consistently follow a method of valuating the ending inventory. Three common methods of valuation are FIFO, LIFO, and weighted average. In times of changing prices, the method a business uses to valuate its ending inventory will influence the amount of net income reported for the accounting period.

1. First In, First Out (FIFO). The FIFO method of valuating inventory assumes that the merchandise is sold in the same order as it was obtained—the first merchandise purchased is the first merchandise sold. Therefore, the merchandise remaining in ending inventory is assumed to be the last items purchased.

a. Learning Outcomes. Students must be able to calculate the dollar value assigned to the ending inventory of a business using the FIFO method.

b. Teaching Methods. Before presenting any of the inventory methods, students must understand *why* the business needs to assign a dollar amount to the ending inventory and *why* the business does not already know this information. The reason a business needs to assign a dollar amount to ending inventory is so that the cost of merchandise sold for that accounting period can be calculated. Remind students that the Merchandise Inventory account does not change during an accounting period. When merchandise is purchased, the Purchases account is debited. When merchandise is sold, the Sales account is credited for the amount of the sale, *not* the *cost of merchandise* sold; therefore, at the end of the fiscal period, neither the cost of the merchandise sold nor or the amount of ending inventory on hand is known.

Review the calculation of the cost of merchandise sold by writing the following on the chalkboard:

```
  Beginning inventory
+ Purchases
  ─────────────────────
  Cost of Mdse. Avail. for Sale
- Ending inventory
  ─────────────────────
  Cost of Merchandise Sold
```

Point out that if the ending inventory could be determined, the cost of merchandise sold could be calculated. Ask students how a business could determine its ending inventory. The desired answer is that the company could count the inventory on hand at the end of the accounting period, which would indicate the *number* of items on hand. However, the business must assign a dollar value to the inventory in order to calculate cost of merchandise sold.

Use an example similar to the one below to explain why the business does not know the *exact* dollar value of inventory.

Example: A store buys 100 pencils at a cost of 5 cents each. Many people want pencils and the store starts running low. The store buys 50 more pencils but has to pay 6 cents for each pencil. At the end of the month, the store counts the number of pencils on hand. There are 45 pencils left. The store knows the *number* of pencils in ending inventory (45), but the dollar value of the pencils is not known. Did the 45 pencils still on hand cost 5 cents or 6 cents?

Explain that the store must follow an acceptable method to determine the dollar value of the 45 pencils. One such method is the First In, First Out or FIFO method. This method assumes that the first pencils purchased were the first pencils sold. Therefore, the 45 pencils remaining in inventory are the last 45 pencils purchased. The dollar value of the 45 pencils would be $2.70.

At this point, emphasize that all inventory methods are based on the *assumption* that the merchandise flows in and out of the company in the stated manner. The merchandise does not have to actually follow this flow. The merchandise in a grocery store may follow the first in, first out, method. (Explain how grocers stock shelves from the back.) Even though the merchandise actually follows a FIFO-type flow, however, the grocery store does *not* have to use the FIFO method of assigning a dollar value to its inventory.

Secondly, emphasize that FIFO flow refers to the merchandise sold, *not* the merchandise left in inventory. The FIFO methods assumes that the first merchandise purchased is the first merchandise sold. Remind students that they need to determine the dollar value of the ending inventory, not the cost of merchandise sold.

Once students understand why a dollar value has to be assigned to the ending inventory, the various methods become easier to understand. To give students practice on the FIFO method, display on the chalkboard or a transparency inventory information similar to Illustration 10–6.

DATE	TRANSACTION	NO. OF UNITS	COST PER UNIT
May 1	Beginning Inventory	30	4.00
7	Purchased	40	4.20
15	Sold	50	
19	Purchased	70	4.35
29	Sold	15	

Illustration 10–6   Inventory Information

Ask students to calculate:

Number of units available	(30 + 40 + 70 = 140)
Number of units sold	(50 + 15 = 65)
Number of units in ending inventory	(140 − 65 = 75)

Ask students to calculate the dollar value of ending inventory using the FIFO method. When students are done, display the following calculations:

```
Ending Inventory:  70 units × 4.35 = 304.50
                    5 units × 4.20 =  21.00
           Totals  75 units          325.50
```

Again, remind students that the FIFO flow is an assumption. The business is *assuming* that the first merchandise in is the first merchandise out. Have students use the FIFO method to calculate ending inventory for several situations. Display and discuss the correct answers.

2. Last In, First Out (LIFO). The LIFO method of valuating inventory assumes that the merchandise is sold in the reverse order as it was obtained — the last merchandise purchased is the first merchandise sold. The merchandise remaining in ending inventory is assumed to be the first items purchased.

a. Learning Outcomes. Students must be able to calculate the dollar value assigned to the ending inventory of a business using the LIFO method.

b. Teaching Methods. The introduction of the Last In, First Out, (LIFO) method should build on the knowledge acquired in the discussion of the FIFO method. Explain that the LIFO method assumes the opposite flow of FIFO in that the last merchandise purchased is the first merchandise sold; therefore, the merchandise remaining in inventory is the first merchandise purchased.

Display the inventory information given in Illustration 10–6.
Ask students to calculate:

Number of units available	(30 + 40 + 70 = 140)
Number of units sold	(50 + 15 = 65)
Number of units in ending inventory	(140 − 65 = 75)

Ask students to calculate the dollar value of ending inventory using the LIFO method. When students are done, display the following calculations:

```
Ending Inventory:  30 units × 4.00 = 120.00
                   40 units × 4.20 = 168.00
                    5 units × 4.35 =  21.75
           Totals  75 units          309.75
```

Again, remind students that the LIFO flow is an assumption. The business is *assuming* that the last merchandise in is the first merchandise out. Have students use the LIFO method to calculate ending inventory for several situations. Display and discuss the correct answers.

3. Weighted Average. The weighted average method of valuating inventory uses the average price paid for merchandise as the basis for assigning a dollar amount to the ending inventory. The average price is calculated at the end of the accounting period.

a. Learning Outcomes. Students must be able to calculate the dollar value assigned to the ending inventory of a business using the weighted average method.

b. Teaching Methods. Explain that in the weighted average method of valuating inventory, an average cost is calculated for each unit. The average cost is then applied to the number of units remaining in inventory to assign a dollar value to the ending inventory. Stress that the average is calculated at the *end* of the accounting period.

Display the inventory information given in Illustration 10–6. Demonstrate how the weighted average is calculated by putting the following information on the chalkboard:

Weighted Average
Merchandise Available for Sale

No. of Units	×	Cost per Unit	=	Total Cost
30	×	4.00	=	120.00
40	×	4.20	=	168.00
70	×	4.35	=	304.50
Totals 140				592.50

$$\text{Weighted Average} = \frac{592.50}{140}$$

$$= 4.23 \text{ per unit}$$

$$\text{Ending Inventory} = 4.23 \times 75 \text{ units}$$

$$= 317.25$$

Point out that the total *cost* of merchandise available for sale is divided by the total *number of units* of merchandise available for sale. The resulting average is then multiplied by the number of units in ending inventory to arrive at the dollar amount assigned to ending inventory. Mention that the weighted average method will assign a dollar amount to inventory that is between the amounts assigned using FIFO and LIFO.

Have students use the weighted average method to calculate ending inventory for several situations. Display and discuss the correct answers.

Comparing Cost of Merchandise Sold Using Different Inventory

Methods. In times of changing prices, the method used to valuate ending inventory will affect the calculation of the cost of merchandise sold reported for the accounting period.

1. Learning Outcomes. Students must understand and be able to state the affect that each inventory method has on the cost of merchandise sold and on the net income reported by the business.

2. Teaching Methods. After discussing the three inventory methods, present the effect of the inventory methods on cost of merchandise sold by calculating cost of merchandise sold using all three methods. Use a side-by-side method similar to Illustration 10–7. Display the results on the chalkboard or a transparency.

	Inventory Costing Method		
Calculation of Cost of Mdse. Sold	FIFO	LIFO	Weighted Average
Beginning Inventory	120.00	120.00	120.00
+ Purchases	472.50	472.50	472.50
Cost of Mdse. Avail. for Sale	592.50	592.50	592.50
– Ending Inventory	325.50	309.75	317.25
Cost of Mdse. Sold	267.00	282.75	275.25

Illustration 10–7 Cost of Merchandise Sold Under Various Inventory Methods

At this point, students should know how to calculate cost of merchandise sold. Therefore, concentrate on the different dollar amounts assigned to ending inventory under the three methods. Point out that using different dollar amounts for ending inventory affects the dollar amount calculated for cost of merchandise sold. Also point out that, in time of rising prices, FIFO results in the lowest cost of merchandise sold and LIFO results in the highest cost of merchandise sold. The weighted average method results in a cost of merchandise sold between that for FIFO and LIFO — an "average" cost of merchandise sold.

Remind students that since cost of merchandise sold affects net income or net loss, the inventory method used does affect the net income or loss reported for the accounting period.

Estimating the Value of Merchandise Inventory–Gross Profit Method.

A business may not always be able to count its inventory in order to assign a dollar value to the ending inventory. In the case of a fire or a theft, the business must estimate the value of its ending inventory for insurance purposes. The gross profit method is a common method used to estimate the dollar value of ending merchandise inventory.

1. Learning Outcomes. Students must be able to calculate the estimated dollar value assigned to the ending inventory of a business using the gross profit method.

2. Teaching Methods. Begin by explaining why a business may not be able to count inventory on hand: (a) Physically counting inventory is time consuming and costly; therefore, many businesses use an estimate for monthly financial statements, only taking the time to actually count inventory once a year. (b) If a business suffers a loss from fire or theft, the business must make an estimate of the inventory on hand before the loss in order to determine the dollar amount of the loss.

Once students understand the need for estimating ending inventory, explain how the amount of inventory is estimated using the gross profit method. Begin by writing the following on the chalkboard or a transparency:

Gross Profit = 35% of Net Sales

The gross profit percentage means that the for every $100.00 of net sales, the business earns $35.00 of gross profit. Explain that a business must calculate its gross profit percentage over several accounting periods to arrive at a reliable average. Once the average gross profit is determined, the accountant uses the average to estimate the average cost of merchandise sold percentage. The formula used is:

100 – Gross Profit Percentage = Cost of Merchandise Sold Percentage

Therefore, cost of merchandise sold percentage is 65% (100 – 35% = 65%). The cost of merchandise sold percentage is used to calculate estimated ending inventory. Students should be familiar with the calculation used to determine the cost of merchandise sold as:

```
  Beginning Inventory
+ Purchases
  ────────────────────
  Cost of Mdse. Available for Sale
− Ending Inventory
  ────────────────────
  Cost of Merchandise Sold
```

Write the calculation on the chalkboard or a transparency. Point out that by interchanging the last two items, the following is obtained:

```
  Cost of Mdse. Available for Sale
− Cost of Mdse. Sold
  ────────────────────
  Ending Inventory
```

Students are now ready for an application of the gross profit method. Write the following on the chalkboard or a transparency:

> The Middleton Company needs to estimate its ending inventory from the available data. An inspection of the financial records indicates the following:
>
> | | |
> |---|---:|
> | Net Sales .... | $7,500.00 |
> | Beginning inventory .... | 4,200.00 |
> | Purchases .... | 6,400.00 |
> | Gross Profit % .... | 30% |

Explain and calculate the following procedure on the chalkboard.

1. Cost of mdse. sold percentage: 100 – 30% =   70%
2. Estimated cost of mdse. sold: 7500 × .70 = 5250
3. Estimated ending inventory:

	Beg. Inv.	4,200
+	Purchases	6,400
	Mdse. Avail. for Sale	10,600
−	Est. Cost of Mdse. Sold	5,250
	Estimated End. Inv.	$5,350

Emphasize that the gross profit method results in an *estimated* ending inventory. In addition, the business must keep track of its gross profit percent from period to period to determine if any adjustment must be made in the average percentage.

Have students use the gross profit method to calculate the estimated ending inventory for several different businesses. Allow students to verify their answers as they finish the calculations.

GENERAL CONSIDERATIONS

Remind students of the purpose of each of the control systems discussed in this chapter. Use bulletin boards to introduce each topic. The bulletin board can consist of the forms, journals, and/or reports used in each control system.

A panel of guest speakers could address the topic of which inventory method produces the most fairly stated financial statements. Use actual inventory items, such as pencils, when introducing the FIFO and LIFO methods of inventory. Get examples of financial statements from local or well-known businesses. Look at the balance sheet to determine how the inventory was valued. Have students read the footnotes to discover disclosure rules for inventory.

Generally, control systems are presented in the second half of the first year or in the second year of accounting instruction when students should have a good basic understanding of journal entries and financial statements. Emphasize the *why* of the procedures to promote understanding rather than memorization.

CHAPTER 11
MEASURING AND EVALUATING LEARNING OUTCOMES

Learning outcomes must be accurately measured and evaluated for several reasons. Feedback of student progress is vital to continued achievement of learning outcomes. As described in Principle 8, Chapter 1, learning proceeds faster when a learner is aware of progress toward desired outcomes. Positive feedback motivates students and builds a foundation for future learning while negative feedback, if used at or very near the time of incorrect action, prevents repeated incorrect performance which hinders future learning. Also, learning is more effective when new learning builds on prior learning, as described in Principle 4, Chapter 1. Learning activities can be more effectively planned when the instructor knows what and how well students have learned. Finally, frequent measurement, in the form of tests, quizzes, and graded assignments, encourages students to thoroughly study and understand each topic as it is introduced.

MEASURING PERFORMANCE

In a competency-based accounting program, the aim of measurement is to gather sufficient performance data to ensure an accurate evaluation of student progress toward predetermined terminal performance objectives. The performance measurement plan must include methods and instruments which adequately measure the three levels of learning in accounting—knowledge, understanding, and application.

Objective-referenced Measurement

In objective-referenced measurement, the learner's performance is compared to a stated terminal performance objective which should guide learning and instruction. The emphasis of objective-referenced measurement should be on learning outcomes. Performance measurement should not simply be an accumulation of data for assigning grades—a required function in most schools.

Learning in accounting is cumulative in nature, building from simple to complex and from the known to the unknown. Terminal performance objectives and performance measurement devices, likewise, should be cumulative in nature. For example, the first stated terminal performance objective may include minimal knowledge, understanding, and application to demonstrate mastery learning levels. A terminal performance objective written for end-of-course performance, however, would require substantially more learning. Objective-referenced measurement, an integral part of planning for instruction, plays a major role in guiding learning and instruction. For example, if the behavior specified in a terminal performance objective is to prepare an income statement, objective-referenced measurement would require preparation of an income statement. A measuring device which asks questions about the purpose and elements of an income statement would *not* be objective-referenced. Learning activities are planned according to the enabling performance tasks necessary to prepare students for successful demonstration of the behavior specified. In developing a performance measurement plan which is objective-referenced, a number of measurement factors must be considered.

Objective Tests

Objective tests typically include true-false, matching, multiple choice, and short-answer questions. Objective tests measure knowledge and understanding of accounting concepts, principles, and procedures. Knowledge of accounting terminology may be measured through matching questions, which require students to match accounting terms with definitions. Understanding of accounting concepts, principles, and procedures may be measured through multiple-choice or other objective-type questions which require students to distinguish between a number of alternatives.

Types of Objective Tests. Objective tests can be used at the end of each chapter to obtain knowledge of results before moving on to the next topic. Objective tests can also be used at the end of a unit, covering several chapters, and can be manually developed. In addition, many textbook publishers offer objective-type exams which can be developed on a microcomputer. Microcomputer exams offer the advantage of quickly and accurately developing multiple versions of the same exam.

Scoring Objective Tests. Objective tests are relatively easy to score. Each question requires one or more simple responses. Points are assigned to each question based on the number of responses required. The general practice is to assign one point for each response. After objective tests are scored, the raw score should be written on each test paper and recorded in the instructor's grade book.

Reporting Test Results. Results on objective tests should be reported as soon as possible after a test is administered. The instructor should review the correct solution for each test question. Although letter grades should not be assigned to individual tests, grade-conscious students will normally pressure the instructor for some indication as to their level of performance on the test. Student anxiety can be overcome by providing tentative grades for the distribution of test scores which can be explained either prior to or after the test has been reviewed. Providing tentative grades will be described later in this chapter. After the test has been reviewed, all copies should be collected and filed for future reference.

Problem Tests and Simulation Audit Tests

Problem tests and simulation audit tests typically measure the application level of accounting learning. Application of accounting concepts, principles, and procedures includes the ability to use learned material in realistic situations and assumes both knowledge and understanding. The application level of learning is measured by the actual performance of a task. For example, measuring students' ability to make journal entries at the application level requires that students actually make the journal entries as part of the test.

Scoring Problem Tests. Problem tests are more difficult to score than objective tests. Requiring a totally correct solution for a complete problem in order for a student to receive any credit is not justifiable. Various scoring approaches can be used. One approach is to either give points for sections of a problem or for each line of a solution. On a work sheet, for example, one point might be assigned for each line that involves the simple extension of amounts to either the income statement columns or the balance sheet columns. Two points might be assigned for lines involving adjustments; two points for column totals based on the actual amounts written in each column; five points for the net income based on each student's column totals; and one point for correct rulings. Assigning points for each line gives students credit for correctly using the amounts entered on the work sheet regardless of whether these amounts are correct or incorrect.

Because of the nature of the problem, some responses may involve prior learning which has been measured before, while other responses involve new learning. More points should be assigned to measurements of new learning.

Scoring Simulation Audit Tests. Completing a business simulation represents application of accounting concepts, principles, and procedures in a realistic situation. Simulation audit tests require short-answer responses to questions about specific information taken from a completed business simulation. Simulation audit tests are relatively easy to score.

Because simulation audit tests require short answers to questions about different parts of a completed simulation, scoring is generally on a point system similar to objective tests. Some instructors also award points for various components of the completed simulation. Points may also be awarded for neatness, accuracy, legibility, rulings, format of financial statements, and/or submitting the simulation when due.

Reporting Test Results. Results on problem and simulation audit tests should be reported as soon as possible after a test is administered. A transparency of the correct solution for a problem test should be reviewed with students. The correct answers for a simulation audit test should be identified and discussed. Although letter grades should not be assigned to individual tests, tentative grades may be assigned to the raw test scores which can be explained either prior to or after the test has been reviewed. This procedure will be described later in this chapter. After the test has been reviewed, all copies should be collected and filed for future reference.

Homework

The topic of homework in accounting is a topic that never fails to generate a discussion. Since homework is a vital element of the accounting learning process, homework should be treated with great importance. If homework is not included in the measurement plan, students are likely to attach little importance to this learning activity. Generally, students who perform well in accounting attribute their success to diligence in doing homework. Success is not just a matter of good luck. However, because the content of the homework will normally be measured as part of the regular formal testing program, the relative weight assigned to homework should be kept low. The challenge to the instructor is to arrive at an appropriate balance between the treatment of homework and the relative weight assigned to the homework. Classes of students with low motivation for homework may need greater incentive. Suggestions for the relative weight to be assigned to the homework are given later in this chapter.

Scoring, Reviewing, and Collecting Homework. After students complete homework, they should be provided with correct solutions through a homework review conducted by the instructor. Homework review allows feedback on the quality of work completed. A transparency of the correct solution is a common device used to review homework. Complexity of the assignment naturally determines the amount of time needed to adequately review homework; however, the review should be completed as quickly as possible.

Each accounting instructor must develop a philosophy regarding the scoring, reviewing and collecting of accounting homework. When developing a homework philosophy, many factors should be considered and many options are available. Factors to be considered include when and how to review homework, when and how to score homework, how often to collect homework, how to limit the copying of homework, how to stress the importance of completing homework, and how much time the instructor should devote to correcting homework.

1. Reviewing homework before homework is scored. Many instructors prefer to review the homework before the homework is scored. Since homework is a learning activity, students may be allowed to make minor corrections on their papers as each phase of the homework is reviewed. This procedure is motivational and enhances learning. Students who discover minor errors in their homework tend to lose interest in the remainder of the review session. If minor errors can be corrected, students will end the review session with a correct solution and a feeling of accomplishment. The instructor must not allow sufficient time during the homework review to permit students to copy major parts of the assignments from the model being displayed. This potential problem can be eliminated by exposing only those portions of the homework being reviewed.

Minor corrections generally include incorrect amounts due to simple mathematical errors or changes in account titles. When students make these minor corrections, they should be required to follow the established rules for making corrections and not be allowed to simply erase incorrect entries except on work sheets. Instructors who accept homework with minor corrections will eliminate the frustrations students often have when they spend many hours trying to locate an error which resulted from a simple mathematical error.

After homework has been reviewed, papers should be collected, scored, and returned during the next class period. Scoring homework can be extremely time consuming. A technique or system should be developed which reduces this task. One technique is outlined on page 129.

1. Only correct solutions (including corrected solutions) may be turned in for scoring. Allowing students to make minor corrections during the homework review vastly reduces the amount of time needed to score homework. The instructor only glances through the papers to be sure all material is included and is truly correct.
2. Homework needing major corrections is due at the beginning of the next class period and is not accepted for credit beyond this date.
3. Point values for each homework assignment are: 10 points for correct solutions turned in on the day due; 7 points for correct solutions turned in the day after the homework review; and 3 points for effort when an assignment is turned in when due and major errors are found during the scoring process. No credit is given for partially completed homework.

This technique places major emphasis on submitting correct homework solutions with some consideration given to sincere effort.

2. Scoring homework before homework is reviewed. Some instructors like to score the homework before it is reviewed, to prevent students from copying the model presented in the review and submitting it as completed homework. One method is for the instructor to walk through the room, checking each student's homework for completeness and recording points attained on the seating chart. This process should take no more than 3-5 minutes. While the instructor is checking off the homework assignments, students can be doing a 5-minute write on what they remember from the topic discussed the previous day (see Chapter 1).

The above technique requires a minimum amount of instructor time and also allows students to correct all errors discovered during the homework review. Since the instructor does *not* collect the homework after the review, students are able to keep the corrected homework problem. The corrected problem can be used as a reference for student study and review. One shortcoming of this method is that the instructor is only checking to determine if the homework has been completed. Accuracy of homework is not graded.

Another method of scoring homework before it is reviewed is to have each student complete a short, oral audit-type quiz. Each student uses a sheet of paper numbered from one to ten. The instructor recites an oral audit-type quiz, such as, "1. What is the net income obtained in Problem 7-2?" Each student records the net income obtained in Problem 7-2. When the homework check is completed, the answer sheets are handed in for scoring by the instructor. Points are awarded for each correct answer. Homework scores are recorded and the sheets can be returned the next day. This technique also uses very little class time and allows students to retain the homework problems to use as a reference for further study and review. A shortcoming of using an audit-type type for checking homework is that only accuracy is checked. Sloppy work is neither identified nor corrected.

3. Group presentation of homework problems. The group method of problem solving works especially well in second-year accounting classes. Homework problems are completed by groups of students, with each group completing the same problem or each group completing a different problem. If each group completes the same problem, one group can be assigned the task of presenting the solution to the class. This method encourages group cooperation and provides practice in public speaking. Students not presenting the solution tend to listen intently as fellow students present the solution. Students presenting the problem solution correctly identify the difficult parts of the assignment and provide the explanation of the correct solution. A group score should be given to each member of the group.

4. Other homework considerations. Students will be encouraged to complete homework assignments if they see a relationship between the content of homework assignments and the major topics included in the formal testing program. If there is a relationship between homework and tests, students will quickly learn that the best way to adequately prepare for a test is to complete and *understand* all homework assignments. The need to understand homework assignments encourages students to complete assignments independently.

Finally, the instructor must determine how many homework assignments to score and how much time should be spent grading homework versus preparing study materials and lesson plans. By trying many different homework plans, the instructor can identify which plan best fits the needs of students and best accomplishes the objectives of the course.

Regardless of the scoring method followed, the system should be thoroughly reviewed with students at the beginning of the course so students know exactly how their homework efforts will be measured.

Informal Measurement

Tests are the basis for a formal performance measurement program. However, informal performance measurement is also vitally important to the total measurement plan. Informal performance measurement is a daily responsibility of an accounting instructor and is accomplished primarily through observation—moving around the room during work sessions, providing assistance, explanations, and on-the-spot instruction.

Informal measurement can also take the form of an assessment check of all students to determine if a previously discussed topic was adequately learned. Some short assessment checks could be:

1. Raise your hand if you can define the word "liabilities."
2. Fill in the elements of the accounting equation:

    A _____ = L _____ + O _____ E _____
3. Brainstorm with other students the various types of liabilities and share your list with the group next to you.

Assessment checks help the instructor to determine if learning can proceed or if more review (or reteaching) must occur first.

Sources of Measuring Instruments

Various measuring instruments are available from the publishers of accounting textbooks. The measuring instruments are correlated with the specific textbook and include objective, problem, and simulation audit tests. Some publishing companies also produce microcomputer exams and/or test banks. Many instructors use these published tests as the primary basis for the performance measurement program. Occasionally, instructors will want to construct their own tests. Good test construction principles and procedures should be followed when developing measurement instruments. Many excellent references are available to assist the instructor in test construction.

EVALUATING PERFORMANCE

A well organized and managed performance measurement plan provides the instructor with the data necessary to evaluate students' progress as well as the instructor's effectiveness. Evaluating performance provides data for grade reporting. Grades are used in most schools as the basis for reporting performance to students, parents, and other interested persons and as a basis for promotion, graduation, and honors.

Even though most school systems only require formal grade reporting at prescribed periods during a school year, accounting instructors must evaluate continually. Performance measurement provides accounting instructors with the data needed to evaluate progress toward desired learning outcomes and to plan activities for new learnings. Evaluation also provides the feedback students need in order to gain from their successes and failures.

Performance Criteria

When students develop skills for employment purposes, evaluation generally is based on two sets of performance criteria—employment standards and grading standards. Criteria for employment are generally based on minimum employment standards while criteria for grading are generally based on overall school standards which apply to all subject-matter areas.

Employment Criteria Versus Grading Criteria. Since the advent of competency-based education, much confusion has existed between the criteria used for employment and the criteria used for grading. Criteria used for employment are generally stated as minimum percentages of accuracy of performance required for obtaining entry-level employment. Employment criteria are generally the minimum level of performance stated in a terminal performance objective. Criteria for grading purposes usually convert the percentages of performance to letter grades.

To set the minimum levels of performance for employment, instructors should use local employment standards based on recommendations from an advisory committee or survey of local businesses. To set the level of performance for grading purposes, instructors should use overall school grading standards. These two sets of performance standards often do not agree. School grading standards are set for all subject-matter areas, not just for subjects which involve skills for entry-level employment. School standards for letter grades may be lower than employment standards. For example, the minimum performance established in a terminal performance objective for a particular task may be 90% accuracy. A student reaching a performance level of 85% accuracy would not have met the minimum established for entry-level employment.

However, criteria established for grade reporting in most schools would likely indicate that a performance of 85% would be above average — more likely a grade of B. A student may perform very well on knowledge and understanding measurement, but is unable to apply this learning to meet entry-level employment standards.

As minimum performance levels for employment are more easily understood by prospective employers when stated in percentages, performance criteria used in terminal performance objectives are based on minimum percentages of accuracy. Likewise, using letters to report grades appears to be more acceptable to students, parents, and counselors. This double standard is likely to continue well into the future. Instructors must clearly explain at the beginning of the course how students will be evaluated for employment purposes and how they will be evaluated for grading purposes.

Grading Criteria. The key to successful grading in accounting is the establishment of valid methods and criteria for evaluating learning in relation to what has been taught. These methods and criteria should be communicated at the beginning of the course.

To report grades, most schools use either a five-point or a twelve-point grading system. The most common version of the five-point system is A B C D E(F). Some schools use E as the lowest grade; some schools use F as the lowest grade. The twelve-point system is simply an extension of the five-point system using plus (+) and minus (−) to provide greater discrimination within each letter grade.

Most grading systems attach a letter grade to a level of performance based on percentages of possible raw-score points available. The level of performance (percentage) is generally fixed. These fixed standards, however, tend to vary from one school to the next since school goals and employment conditions vary. Suggested grading criteria for both a five-point and a twelve-point system are provided in Illustration 11–1.

FIVE-POINT SYSTEM		TWELVE-POINT SYSTEM	
Letter Grade	Percent	Letter Grade	Percent
		A+ =	98 – 100
A =	90 – 100	A =	93 – 97
		A− =	90 – 92
		B+ =	87 – 89
B =	80 – 89	B =	83 – 86
		B− =	80 – 82
		C+ =	77 – 79
C =	70 – 79	C =	73 – 76
		C− =	70 – 72
		D+ =	67 – 69
D =	60 – 69	D =	63 – 66
		D− =	60 – 62
E(F) =	Below 60	E(F) =	Below 60

Illustration 11–1 Grading Criteria

The grading criteria in Illustration 11-1 provide for a 10-point spread in each grade level with the exception of the grade of A. The grade of A has an 11-point spread in order to include 100%. Schools which do not include an A+ grade in their grading system usually divide the 90–100 percentage range between A and A− grades— A− = 90–94%; A = 95–100%.

Either the five-point or the twelve-point system may be used; however, the twelve-point system is recommended because it allows a clearer distinction between the various levels of performance. For example, performance of 89 and 80% would be assigned the same letter grade in the five-point system—a grade of B. In the twelve-point system, performance of 89% is a B+ grade and 80% is a B− grade.

Relative Weighting of Measurement Factors

Different weights may be placed on each measurement factor. However, the weight assigned to each factor should reflect the level of learning measured by that factor. For example, knowledge represents the lowest level of learning; therefore, factors which measure knowledge should be assigned a relative weight less than a factor which measures understanding. Suggested relative weights for the measurement factors discussed in this chapter are given in Illustration 11-2.

Factors	Weights
Objective tests	30 percent
Problem tests	40 percent
Simulation audit tests	20 percent
Homework	10 percent

Illustration 11-2 Relative Weights for Measurement Factors

The recommended relative weights for each of the performance measurement factors take into consideration the three levels of learning. Learning outcomes which demonstrate knowledge involve recall of previously learned subject matter. Being able to identify the correct definition of an accounting term is an example of a learning outcome which demonstrates knowledge. Understanding goes one step beyond the simple remembering of material and assumes the knowledge level of learning. Learning outcomes which demonstrate understanding involve the ability to interpret subject matter. Being able to distinguish between correct and incorrect accounting principles and practices is an example of a learning outcome which demonstrates understanding. Application represents a higher level of learning than either knowledge or understanding and assumes both. Learning outcomes which demonstrate application involve the ability to use learned material in realistic situations. Being able to record transactions in a journal is an example of a learning outcome which demonstrates application.

Reporting Progress Grades

Even though performance on each individual performance measurement device is generally reported as a raw score rather than a letter grade, students should be informed of their relative progress toward established grading criteria after each performance measurement. One method used to report this progress is to include both a raw score for the individual measurement plus an accumulated raw score for all performance measurements to date on each performance measurement paper returned.

Data in a format similar to Illustration 11–3 are placed on a transparency or chalkboard and reviewed with students after each performance measurement. Illustration 11–3 shows the grade range for raw scores for two performance measurements. The distribution of raw scores in each grade range is determined by the grading criteria, Illustration 11–1. For example, the possible points for Test 1, 50, is multiplied by 90% to determine the lower end of the A grade range, 45. Students find the grade range for their raw scores on the table and receive immediate feedback as to their progress toward established grading criteria. For example, a student who scored 43 (high B range) on the first test and 57 (middle A range) on the second test has an accumulated raw score of 100 (low A range).

Test 1 Possible points 50		Test 2 Possible points 60		Tests 1 & 2 Possible points 110	
Distribution of Raw Scores	Grade Range	Distribution of Raw Scores	Grade Range	Distribution of Accumulated Raw Scores	Grade Range
45 – 50	A	54 – 60	A	99 – 110	A
40 – 44	B	48 – 53	B	88 – 98	B
35 – 39	C	42 – 47	C	77 – 87	C
30 – 34	D	36 – 41	D	66 – 76	D
Below 30	E(F)	Below 36	E(F)	Below 66	E(F)

Illustration 11–3   Reporting Progress Grades

Assigning Interim and Final Grades

Grade reporting periods vary among schools. Some schools operate on a quarter system and some operate on a semester system. Many schools which operate on a semester system require interim grades to be reported at the end of the first nine weeks of each semester. A few schools require interim grade reports each six weeks. Regardless of the grade reporting period used, accounting instructors can ease the burden of formal grade reporting if the measurement and evaluation procedures suggested and described earlier in this chapter are followed.

Throughout the grading period, raw scores should be accumulated for each measurement factor. For example, homework points should be accumulated throughout the grading period. At the end of the grading period, the scores achieved for each measurement factor should be stated in terms of a percentage of possible points for that factor. For example, if a student achieved 95 out of 125 total homework points, that student's homework percentage would be 76% ((95/125) × 100). A percentage of total possible points should be calculated for each measurement factor.

Once a percentage is calculated for each measurement factor, it is multiplied by the relative weight for that specific factor to determine a numeric value. The numeric value for each factor is then added to get a numeric grade for each student. The numeric grade is then compared to the table in Illustration 11–1 to determine a letter grade for each student.

As an example, assume Student A has obtained the following points for each measurement factor:

Objective tests	253 out of 330 points
Problem tests	690 out of 770 points
Simulation audit tests	92 out of 100 points
Homework	95 out of 125 points

To calculate a letter grade for Student A, four steps are followed:

1. Determine the percentage score for each measurement factor.

Objective tests	= 76.7%
Problem tests	= 89.6%
Simulation audit tests	= 92.0%
Homework	= 76.0%

2. Using the relative weights given in Illustration 11–2, multiply the percentage score for each measurement factor times the relative weight for that factor to determine a numeric value.

Objective tests:	.30 × 76.7 = 23.01
Problem tests:	.40 × 89.6 = 35.84
Simulation audit tests:	.20 × 92.0 = 18.40
Homework:	.10 × 76.0 = 7.60

3. Add the numeric values to determine a numeric grade.

Objective tests numeric value	23.01
Problem tests numeric value	35.84
Simulation audit tests numeric value	18.40
Homework numeric value	7.60
Numeric grade	84.85

4. Using Illustration 11–1, transpose the numeric grade to a letter grade.

Interim or final grade = B

Student A's letter grade for the period is a B.

Grading Variations and Abnormal Distributions for Interim Grades

The previous discussion on assigning grades is effective in most situations. At some point, however, most accounting instructors will have to address the problem of test results which do not fit neatly into pre-established grading criteria. For example, what should be done when the top score is 85%? Alternative grading procedures may have to be followed.

Adjusting Unusual Test Scores to Fit Pre-established Criteria. When test scores result in inappropriate grades, the instructor must alter the procedure followed to assign interim grades for that test. Length of test, complexity, and shortage of time can cause unusual test scores. In addition, students may not have been adequately prepared for the test, which may indicate that additional teaching time is necessary. One alternative method is discussed below.

Assume the following distribution of raw scores on a 100–point test:

```
85 – I            72 –
84 –              71 –
83 – II           70 – III
82 – II           69 – I
81 –              68 – I
80 –              67 –
79 – III          66 – I
78 – I            65 –
77 – II           64 –
76 –              63 – I
75 – II           62 –
74 – I            61 – I
73 – I
```

One method of assigning an adjusted test grade is to equate the top test score with the top grade (100) and the middle test score with the "average" grade (assumed to be the lowest B–, or an 80). Since there are 23 student scores in the example, the twelfth score, 75, is the midpoint or middle score. The middle score of 75 should be assigned a grade of 80. The difference between the middle score (75) and the highest score attained (85) must be determined. In this example, the difference between the highest score and the middle score is 10. The difference between the highest grade assigned (100) and the average grade (80) should be determined. The difference is 20.

Next, divide the difference between the highest grade and the average grade, (20) by the difference between the highest score and the middle score, (10). This gives an answer of 2. The grade for each test score below 85 is determined by subtracting 2 grade points from 100 for each point the score is below 85. For example, if a score is 82, it is 3 points below the top score (85). Multiply this difference by 2. This product (6) is subtracted from the highest grade (100), giving this student an adjusted grade of 94 on the test. Column 2 in Illustration 11–4 lists the adjusted grade assignments for every test score.

COLUMN 1 RAW SCORE	COLUMN 2 ADJUSTED SCORE
85 – I	100
84 –	98
83 – II	96
82 – II	94
81 –	92
80 –	90
79 – III	88
78 – I	86
77 – II	84
76 –	82
75 – II	80
74 – I	78
73 – I	76
72 –	74
71 –	72
70 – III	70
69 – I	68
68 – I	66
67 –	64
66 – I	62
65 –	60
64 –	58
63 – I	56
62 –	54
61 – I	52

Illustration 11–4   Adjusted Grade Assignments

The adjusted grades can be entered in the gradebook and treated as any other evaluation score.

Variations of Alternative Grading Procedures.   In the previous example, an average grade of 80 was assigned to the middle test score and the top grade of 100 was assigned to the top test score. For a variety of reasons, this procedure may not be appropriate. The instructor may feel, for example, that the top score (85) does not deserve the top grade of 100. In that situation, the instructor can assign the top grade of 100 to the highest score that could reasonably be expected.

Other variations are:

1. Assign the top grade (100) to the top score and assign the lowest passing grade (60) to the lowest score. This method results in all test scores being assigned a passing grade.

2. Assign the top grade (100) to the highest score and assign the lowest passing grade (60) to the lowest acceptable passing score.
3. Assign the top grade (100) to the highest reasonably expected score and assign the lowest passing grade (60) to the lowest acceptable passing score.

Regardless of the variation used, the rest of the grade calculations would continue as previously illustrated.

Adjusting Grades for Natural Breaks in Distribution. When assigning grades, the instructor should also examine the overall distribution before strictly applying the pre-established letter grade breaks. Natural breaks in the distribution should be considered. For example, assume the partial distribution of scores given in Illustration 11-5.

DISTRIBUTION	PRE-ESTABLISHED GRADE	ADJUSTED GRADE
98% – II	A	A
95% – I	A	A
94% – I	A	A
93% – I	A	A
90% – III	A	A
89% – II	B	A
86% – II	B	B

Illustration 11-5 Partial Distribution of Scores

A natural break occurs between 86% and 89%. Even though 89% would be a B+ grade based on pre-established grading criteria, natural distribution breaks indicate that 89% should be assigned an A grade. Illustration 11-5 lists the adjusted grades based on natural distribution. Distribution can be considered when assigning interim or final grades.

Whenever deviating from pre-established grading procedures, the accounting instructor must use good judgement in assessing the reasons for the unusual test scores and in determining which variation will result in the assignment of fair grades.

GENERAL CONSIDERATIONS

The suggested procedures outlined and described in this chapter are intended to assist the accounting instructor in designing an accurate and valid measurement and evaluation plan. In designing such a plan, the following guides should be considered:

1. Determine factors to be measured and evaluated and establish appropriate relative weights for each factor.
2. Use methods and instruments to measure knowledge, understanding, and application of accounting concepts, principles, and procedures.

3. Use objective-referenced measurement devices.
4. Develop a grading plan to evaluate performance measurement data which is systematic and accurate.
5. Communicate measurement and evaluation procedures early in the learning process.
6. Gather sufficient data to ensure an accurate evaluation of student progress toward predetermined terminal performance objectives.

Cooperative learning methods can be applied to measurement and evaluation. See Chapter 1 for more information on cooperative learning.

Finally, studies show that frequent and varied measurement activities are more likely to keep students focused on the topics being studied than infrequent or unvarying measurement activities. Using a variety of measurement factors can also compensate for different learning styles discussed in Chapter 1.

Hopefully this text has helped you prepare for effective accounting instruction and given you confidence as you approach your teaching opportunities. As you continue to implement more ideas into each day's lesson, do not forget your colleagues in your own building. Whether in business education or some other area of education, fellow instructors can be good sources of ideas and can help in a problem-solving role. Asking for help and suggestions is not an indication of a lack of ability. It is instead a mark of an interested, caring instructor who is constantly striving to improve and is resourceful enough to tap all resources available.

INDEX

A

Account
    adjustments, general ledger, analyzing, 63-69
    balances, identifying, 35
    balance side of, 36
    contra, 67
    controlling, 49, 56-57
    decreases, identifying, 35-39
    increases, identifying, 35-39
    needing to be closed, identifying, 90-92
    needing to be reversed, identifying, 96-98
Accountants, 29
Account forms
    analysis of, 23
Accounting
    activities, teaching, 21
    advancement-level jobs, 2
    automated, 100
    business simulation, 18
    career ladder, 2
    college preparation for, 4
    competency-based education (CBE) for, 8
    enabling performance tasks for, 11
    entry-level jobs, 1
    evaluation techniques for, 7
    general behavioral goals, 8
    instructional delivery system, 11-14
    general education for, 3
    learning activities, 11
    objective-referenced tests for, 14
    occupational preparation, 1
    performance measurement of, 125
    personal use, 3
    planning for instruction, 7
    principles of effective instruction, 4-7
    program goals for, 8
    study guides, 18
    terminal performance objectives, 10
    textbooks, 17
    tutorials, 18
    workbooks, 18
    working papers, 18
Accounting concepts
    accounting period cycle, 13
    adequate disclosure, 13
    business entity, 13
    consistent reporting, 13
    going concern, 13
    historical cost, 13
    matching expenses with revenue, 13
    materiality, 14
    objective evidence, 13
    realization of revenue, 14
    unit of measurement, 13
Accounting control systems
    essential elements, 109-124
    importance of, 109
    inventory system, 118
    payroll system, 109
    voucher system, 116
Accounting equation, 31-35; *illus.*, 32
    classifying data in, 31
Accounting instruction
    activities for, 21-26
    equipment for, 26-27
    general behavioral goals, 8-10
    integrating computers into, 100-101
    materials for, 17-21
    objectives of, 1-4
    planning for effective, 7-14
    principles of effective, 4-7
    program goals, 8
    sources for help, 27-30
    terminal performance goals, 10-11
Accounting instructors, resources for, 27-30
Accounting period cycle concept, 13
Accounts, chart of, 53-56
    general ledger, 53
Accrued expenses, adjustment for, 73
Accrued revenue, adjustment for, 74
Accuracy, checking of, in journals, 50-51
Activities, 21
Adequate disclosure concept, 13
Adjusting entries, 61
    importance of, 61
    journalizing, 89
Adjustments, 61
    accrued expenses, 73
    accrued revenue, 74
    analysis, 63
    columns on a work sheet, 75
    contra accounts, 67

general ledger accounts, 63-69
  identifying accounts in need of, 63
  merchandise inventory, 65
  planning, on work sheet, 74
  prepaid expense
    recorded initially as
      expense, 69
  unearned revenue
    recorded initially as liability, 70
    recorded initially as revenue, 71
Advancement-level jobs, 2
Advisory committee, 29
American Institute of Certified Public
  Accountants, 29
American Society of Women
  Accountants, 19
Asset, 32
  adjustment for prepaid expense
    recorded initially as, 69
  in accounting equation, 33-39

B

Balance sheet
  columns of a work sheet, 80, 82;
    illus., 84
  preparing, 83-85
Balance side of account, 38
Balance, trial, recording on a worksheet,
  61-62
Bulletin boards, 27
Business entity concept, 13
Business simulations, 18
  audit tests, 126

C

Calculators, 27
Capital
  account; *illus.*, 39
  owners, 38-39
Career exploration, 25
Career ladder, 2
Case studies, 20
Cash transactions, recording in check
  register, 117
Chalkboard, 26
Chart of accounts, 53-57
  constructing, 53-56
  general ledger, 53-55
  subsidiary ledgers, 55-57
Check register, recording cash
  transactions in, 117

Closing entries
  analyzing, 92-95
  importance of, 91
  journalizing, 95
College preparation for accounting, 4
Combination journal, 48
Community service, 3-4
Competency-based education (CBE), 8
  model for, 9
Computerized accounting activities,
  evaluation, 108
Computerized problems, 19
Computers, 27
  classroom set up for, 106
  group vs. individual work, 107
  hardware configuration, 106
  instructor's role, 107
  integrating into accounting
    instruction, 100-101
Consistent reporting concept, 13
Contra accounts, 67-69
Controlling account, 49, 55-56
Cooperative learning, 15
Cost of merchandise sold, comparing,
  using different inventories, 121-222
Credit
  debit and, analysis, 39
  importance of, 36
  debit and, in each transaction, 36-38

D

Debit
  credit and, analysis, 39
  importance of, 36
  credit and, in each transaction, 36-38
Debts, bad, 67-69
Delta Pi Epsilon, 28
Demonstration problems, 20
Department of Education, 28
Depreciation, 67-69
Document number column, 45

E

Earnings
  employee record of, 109, 113; *illus.*,
    114
  figuring, from time card, 109-111
Educational software
  application problems, 101-102
  practice sets, 102
  simulations, 102

types of, 101-103
Electronic bulletin boards, 30
Employee earnings record, 109; *illus.*, 114
Employer payroll taxes, 115-116
Employment criteria, 131
Enabling performance tasks, 11
   relationship between goals, objectives, and, *illus.*, 12
End-of-fiscal-period work, 61-78
Entries
   closing, analyzing, 92-95
   closing, journalizing, 95-96
   reversing, journalizing, 98-99
Entry level jobs, 1
Equation, accounting, 31-35; *illus.*, 32
   classifying data in, 31
Equipment, adjustment for, 67-69
Equity, 32
Evaluation techniques for accounting, 21
Evaluative tools, 21
Expenses
   accrued, adjustment for, 73-74
   prepaid, adjustment for, 63; *illus.*, 65
   recorded initially as expense, 69

F

Federal income tax, 111
Federal unemployment tax, 115-116
FICA tax
   employer, 115
   figuring employee, 111
Field trips, 23
Final grades, assigning, 134-135
Financial data, classifying, 31-33
Financial statements
   analysis of, 85
   balance sheet, 83
   importance of, 79
   income statement, 79
   stockholders' equity statement, 82
Flash cards, 22
Form analysis, 23; *illus.*, 24

G

Games, 22
General behavioral goals for accounting, 8
   relationship between, objectives, and tasks, *illus.*, 12

General journal, 45
   multi-column, 46
   payroll taxes expense in, 115
General ledger accounts, 53
   adjustments, 63-69
   posting to, 58; *illus.*, 58
General ledger charts of accounts, 53-55; *illus.*, 54
Gifted students, 16
Going concern concept, 13
Grades
   abnormal distributions, 136-138
   assigning interim and final, 134
   reporting to students, 133
   variations, 136-138
Grading criteria, 132
Guest speakers, 25

H

Historical cost concept, 13
Homework, 127-130
   assignment, 14
   review, 12, 128
   scoring, 128
Hypergraphics, 20

I

Income, net
   figuring on work sheet, 80-82; *illus.*, 80
   on income statement, 81; *illus.*, 80
Income statement
   columns on work sheet, *illus.*, 80
   cost of merchandise sold on, 81
   preparing, 79-81
Instructional delivery system, 111
Inventory system, 118-121

J

Journal
   checking accuracy of, 50
   combination, 48
   common features of, 44-45
   document number column on, 45
   expanded multi-column, 48
   general, 45-46
   importance of, 44
   multi-column, 46, 48
   posting, 57-58, 67-70
   ruling, 51

special, 49
special amount column on, 46
totaling, 51
two-column general, 45
Journalizing, 44

L

Learning activities, 11-14
Learning outcomes
   accounting control systems, 109
   payroll system, 109
   voucher system, 116
   accounting equation, 31
   adjusting entries, 61
   analysis of adjustments, 63
   closing entries, 91
   competency-based education for, 8
   debit/credit analysis, 35
   financial statements, 79
   journalizing, 44
   journals, 44
   ledgers, 53
   measurement of, 125
   posting, 53
   reversing entries, 96
   transaction analysis, 31
   work sheets, 61
Learning principles, 4-7
Learning styles, 14-15
Ledger accounts
   adjustments, 63-74
   identify, needing adjustment, 63
   posting to, 57-58
Ledgers, 53
   posting to, 58
Liabilities, 31-38
   adjustment for unearned revenue, 70-71
Loss, net, 79-81
   figuring on work sheet, 81

M

Matching expenses with revenue concept, 13
Materiality concept, 14
Measurement factors, relative weighting of, 133
Mentoring, 25
Merchandise inventory
   adjustments for, 65
   gross, estimating value of, 122-124
Merchandise sold, cost of, comparing, using different inventories, 121-122
Motivational aids, miscellaneous, 21

N

National Business Education Association, 28
National Society of Public Accountants, 29
Net income, 79-81
Net loss, 79-81
Normal account balances, identifying, 35-39

O

Objective evidence concept, 13
Objective-referenced measurement, 125
Objective referenced test, 14
Objective test, 21, 126
   reporting results, 126
   scoring, 126
Occupational preparation, 1
   for accounting career, 1-2
   related, 3-4
Overhead projector, 26
   positioning of, in classroom, 26
Owners' equity, 31
   statement, preparing, 82-83

P

Paper and pencil activities, 23
Payroll, computerized programs, 103
Payroll register, 111
Payroll system, 109-116
   importance of, 109
Payroll taxes, 115
   employer figuring, 115
   journalizing, 115
   posting, 115
Payroll time card, 109
   figuring employee earnings from, 109
Payroll transactions
   analyzing, 115
   journalizing, 115
   posting, 115
Performance criteria
   employment, 131
   grading, 132

reporting students progress towards, 133
Performance evaluation, 131-138
  assigning interim and final grades, 134
  reporting progress grades to students, 133
Performance measurement
  homework, 127
  informal measurement, 130
  measuring instruments, 130-131
  objective-referenced measurement, 125-126
  objective tests, 126
  problem tests, 126-127
  simulation audit tests, 126-127
Planning for instruction, 7
Posting
  importance of, 53
  journals, 57-60
Prepaid expenses
  adjustments for, 63; *illus*., 65
  recorded initially as expense, 69
Principles of effective instruction, 4-7
Problem tests, 21, 126
  reporting results, 127
  scoring, 127
Professional business teacher associations, 28
Professional journals, 30
Program goals for accounting, 8
Progress grades
  assigning interim and final, 134
  criteria for, 132
  reporting to students, 133
Publishing companies, 28

R

Realization of revenue concept, 14
Resources, 17
Revenue
  accrued, adjustment for, 73
  unearned
    recorded initially as liability, 70
    recorded initially as revenue, 71
Reversing entries, 96
  journalizing, 98-99
Ruling journals, 51

S

Service organizations, 29

Shadowing, 25
Simulations, business, 18
  audit tests, 126
  educational software, 102
Software, choosing, 103-106
Special amount columns, 47
Special journals, 49
Special needs students, mainstreaming of, 15-16
Spreadsheets, 102
Stockholders' equity statement, 82-83
Student clubs, accounting for, 25
Study groups, 25
Study guides, 18
Subsidiary ledgers, 55-57

T

T accounts, 36-39
Tax
  federal income, 111
  federal unemployment, 115-116
  FICA, 111, 115
  state unemployment, 116
Teaching methods
  accounting control systems, 109
  accounting equation, 31
  adjustment entries, 61
  analysis of adjustments, 63
  closing entries, 91
  debit/credit analysis, 36
  financial statements, 79
  homework, 11-12, 127
  journalizing, 44
  journals, 44
  ledgers, 53
  payroll system, 109
  posting, 57
  reversing entries, 96
  transaction analysis, 31-32, 33-35, 36-39, 40-42
  voucher system, 116
  work sheets, 61
Teaching strategies, 14-16
Teaching styles, 14-15
Terminal performance objectives, 10-11
  relationship between goals, and tasks, illus., 12
Testing instruments
  objective tests, 126
  problem test, 126
  selection of, 130-131
  simulation audit tests, 126

Textbooks, 17
Time card
   figuring employee earning from, 109; *illus.*, 110
Totaling journals, 51
Transaction analysis, 31
Transactions
   analyzing, 33
   effects of, on the accounting equation, 33
   into debit and credit parts, 35
   journalizing in a general journal, 45
   journalizing in a multi-column journal, 46-49
   journalizing in a special journal, 49-50
   using T accounts, 36-39
Transparencies, overhead projector, 20
Trial balance
   columns of work sheet, 61
   recording on work sheet, 61
Tutorials, 18

U

Unearned revenue, 70
   adjustment for
      recorded initially as liability, 70
      recorded initially as revenue, 71
Unemployment tax payable - federal, 115-116
Unemployment tax payable - state, 116
Unit of measurement concept, 13

V

Value of merchandise inventory, gross, estimating, 122-124
Voucher register, 116
Voucher system, 116-118
   importance of, 116

W

Wall charts, 27
Whiteboard, 26
Withholding taxes, 111, 115-116
Workbooks, 18
Working papers, 18
Work sheet
   balance sheet columns, *illus.*, 80
   completing, 75
   figuring net income or net loss on, 81
   form analysis, 24
   importance of, 80
   income statement columns, *illus.*, 80
   planning adjustments, 74-75
   recording trial balance, 61-62
   trial balance columns, 61
   used in preparing
      balance sheet, 83-85
      income statement, 79